Fifty Tea Bags and a Bottle of Rum

Fifty Tea Bags and a Bottle of Rum

NICK COWAN

QUARTET

First published in 2008 by
Quartet Books Limited
A member of the Namara Group
27 Goodge Street, London WIT 2LD

A catalogue record for this book
is available from the British Library

ISBN   978 0 7043 7144 6

Typeset by Antony Gray
Printed and bound in Great Britain by
T J International Ltd, Padstow, Cornwall

To the memory of

D.J.C. and D.C.

Contents

Acknowledgements

Thanks to Caroline Clegg, Julie Cowan, Joanna Doniger, David Giles, Ian Ross, Anthony Speelman and Anthony Vincent all of whom shared some of my experiences to a greater or lesser degree and helped with this book.

Thanks also to Andrea von Stumm, to my editor Hugh Griffith and to Chris Cowan for inspiration for the title.

Introduction

Looking back over the past forty years, I'm led to wonder how, starting from a conventional background, I made a career that brought me into close contact with some of the biggest names in the world of entertainment. It was certainly never part of my life's plan to become a lawyer to the stars, escort agency proprietor, roller-disco operator, record company president or movie producer.

If there is a simple answer, it lies in a natural tendency to gamble. I like to take a chance on whatever comes my way, often saying yes to new opportunities when a more prudent response might be to let them pass. Ever since early days at school I've found the unpredictable road more alluring than the one I already know. The result has been something of a switchback existence, from a huge win that put me in the *Guinness Book of Records* to imminent total wipe-out.

Quite why my father got it into his head that Eton College was a suitable place for me to go to school I have no idea. Although he spent his working life as a dentist in London, both he and my mother were born and died in Dublin, and I spent my childhood holidays with my grandmother, who was part of the small Jewish community in Ireland.

When I arrived for my first term at Eton I knew nobody. I came from an unknown preparatory school, long since closed down, which had never sent anyone to Eton before me. It seemed as if all the other new boys around me had some connection with the place. Most were from rich upper-class families; many were titled. As for the language, Eton has a vocabulary all its own, and while the other boys in my year had a good grounding in this patois I couldn't understand a word of it. Speaking with something of an Irish accent I felt entirely out of place.

Merciless teasing quite naturally followed, until I found I had an aptitude for boxing and made it into the school team. At which point I began to make a circle of friends, many of whom had a material effect on my later life. The mainstream of Eton life was not for me, but one of the joys of that school is the scope it offers for individualism as one becomes more senior. I was seldom to be found exerting myself in an eight on the river or on the playing fields, but spent happy hours painting away in the art department or making a guitar in the mechanical workshops.

Battle was regularly joined over the prescribed norms of appearance and conduct. My housemaster once addressed the entire house, in tones fitted for the denunciation of an appalling crime: 'It has been reported to me that there is a boy in my house who has been seen wearing electric blue socks.' He also wrote to my father, 'I have removed a flick-knife from him but wonder if perhaps he has only surrendered his second-best one.'

I had my first taste of gambling when I subscribed to a tipping service called Epsom Gem Specials. A stream of losing tips soon convinced me that being the bookmaker was a better option than being the punter. I found a partner in crime and we began to take bets from a few trusted racing fans. Things went well for a while until Sir William Piggott-Brown started to bet with us. His stepfather was a racehorse trainer and William later went on to become champion amateur jockey in England. There was nothing he didn't know about the racing game and a series of winning bets cleaned us out. In the end I had to pay him in squash racquets which I was able to get from the school shop and charge to the school bill. As I had little interest in squash, or any other sport for that matter, my father was understandably mystified that I was going through racquets at such a rate.

I also fancied myself as an actor, and was cast in the school production of *Gaslight* as the murderous husband who tries to drive his wife insane by raising and lowering the gas lamps. The reviewer in the *Eton College Chronicle* wrote as follows: 'Cowan, finely cast as a super criminal, revealed to us his sinister nature long before the playwright chose to let us into the secret officially.'

The cinema in Windsor was out of bounds but I managed to sneak out to see Little Richard in *The Girl Can't Help It*, my first taste of rock 'n' roll. The local record shop then became my preferred choice as a place to hang out, and my earliest purchase was Elvis Presley's first album. I built up a collection of jazz and rock albums and, much to the annoyance of my neighbours, started playing the trombone.

Between those contemporaries who became lifelong friends there is a connecting thread which runs through to the present. Peregrine Eliot, the Earl of St Germans, was to introduce me to record producer Denny Cordell, which resulted in my spending twenty years in the US. Jonathan Irwin, who was a new boy in my house at the same time as me, became the owner of Sandymount House in Ireland, which I brokered for Ronnie Wood who now lives there. Its previous owner was Lord 'Grey' Gowrie, who as editor of the *Chronicle* had once praised my oil paintings in the annual art exhibition, ascribing to my landscapes the unusual combination of 'Van Gogh's texture, Cézanne's composition and Cowan's colour'.

By the time I came to leave Eton I knew more about horse-racing, poker, alcohol and tobacco than any of my A-level examination subjects. I also had an extensive record collection and no idea what to do next.

My father had always impressed upon me the importance of having a learned profession. As neither medicine nor accountancy had much appeal for me, I turned to the law and enrolled as an articled clerk with a firm of solicitors, Withers & Co. The five years of articles included eighteen months study leave at the College of Law in Lancaster Gate in London, but there seemed little point in wasting time at lectures when so much more could be achieved in afternoons of diligent study in the local betting shop.

As an Etonian, my name inevitably appeared on the list of young men regarded as suitable escorts for the London debutante season – though to the mothers, 'suitable' was hardly the right word for the son of a dentist whose favourite hobbies were gambling and drinking. Invitations to an unvarying sequence of cocktail parties, dances and dinner parties came regularly through the letter-box. The objective of most of the young men, including myself, was to consume as much alcohol as possible, in as little time as possible, before trying to grope whichever unfortunate girls had the pleasure of our company for the evening.

It was during this time that I met my wife-to-be Caroline, when her parents gave her a dance at their home in Cheshire. Her father was a keen hunting man, and this led me during the function into a confrontation with Nigel Dempster, later to become the celebrated society columnist. In the early hours of the morning Nigel decided it would be amusing to let the horses out of their stables with a view to riding one into the marquee where the dance was taking place. My future father-in-law was appalled to find that his best hunter, which was recovering from an operation, had been released from the stables and had got loose on the road. A heated argument ensued, which soon became a fist fight between Nigel and myself. I soon flattened him, but as he slunk away with a bloodied nose his parting words were: 'Just you wait until round two.' From then on I always called him Round Two. In the course of time we became good friends.

Looking back I can see that my generation was fortunate to have had it all on a plate. London in the late '60s and early '70s was the greatest fun imaginable. Jobs and careers were relatively easy to come by, and the old school tie and connections were still hugely influential and helpful. All the partners in Withers & Co. were Old Etonians and I could easily have spent the rest of my days there. Instead, soon after marrying Caroline I joined a law firm of a very different kind, headed by her cousin David Jacobs. Within a few months I was representing John Lennon and Yoko Ono on drugs charges. This, I could see already, was my kind of life.

In at the Deep End

No more than a mile from each other, and both in the West End of London, are 20 Essex Street and 55 Pall Mall, but the two firms of lawyers which occupied premises at these addresses in 1960 were light years apart in their dealings with the law.

Withers & Co., where I started my working life, was a staid firm with a large clientele of titled and landed families. The senior partner, Arthur Collins, was a singularly repulsive-looking figure, who by all accounts had managed to whittle away sizeable chunks of the vast fortunes that many of these families had accumulated over generations. Nevertheless they had nobly absorbed these setbacks without too many complaints, and my life was confined to tying up bundles of documents with pink silk ribbon in the prescribed manner as previous generations of clerks had done.

My conversations with the senior partner were infrequent and almost always brief. One winter morning I arrived in the office wearing a pair of elastic-sided boots. Giving them a horrified look, he spared me only enough time to splutter 'Shoes have laces!' before turning back to the mundane tasks of forming trusts and applying for probate. Criminal law was considered beneath the firm's dignity. Divorce proceedings were handled, since they often affected some of the clients' land and property holdings, but litigation was beyond the pale.

In 55 Pall Mall was housed a law firm of a very different nature. M. A. Jacobs and Sons specialised in the field of entertainment. Its clients consisted of actors, rock groups, theatrical agents, music managers and performers from every aspect of show business. The senior partner, David Jacobs, was a flamboyant character who never missed the first night of any theatrical opening. He lunched every day at the same table at the Caprice in St James's Street around the corner from the office, in the company of one or other of his clients. Celebrities were always welcome guests and the client list bulged with names that appeared regularly in the press.

David was the archetypal tall, dark, handsome man. His hair was jet black, perhaps suspiciously dark for a man in his late fifties. Always immaculately dressed, he was also homosexual – a fact which was known in the office and amongst most of the clients, though he in no way flaunted it. More importantly, so far as I was concerned, he was my wife's cousin, and after we had got married he invited me to join the firm as his sole partner. His brother Jack was named as a partner on the letterhead but played no part in running the firm. I immediately accepted his offer and left Withers with few regrets.

The theatrical world which provided so many of David's clients had a relatively high gay population, and in those days before 1967, the year when sex between consenting gay adults was decriminalised, cases of blackmail were rife. David had a reputation for dealing with the more difficult cases, where the livelihoods of some celebrities were jeopardised by their excursions into the seamier side of theatrical life.

The office at 55 Pall Mall was on three floors and employed some twenty people. Most of the routine work, such as conveyancing, wills, trusts and probate, was done by specialist managing clerks, although David would always meet the client initially. But his speciality was handling the celebrities, whether actors, directors, singers or any others whose names were familiar in the gossip columns of the tabloid press.

In the centre of the offices was the reception area; Sheila, the receptionist, had worked there for many years and knew most of the clients. And many of them knew each other. I would walk through the reception area and see them eyeing each other and clearly thinking, 'I wonder what he's doing here. Could he be in the same sort of mess I'm in?' Gay blackmail cases were settled in all kinds of ways. Frequently the celebrity involved was reluctant to go to the police and fearful of public exposure. Often a sum of money would change hands, but I soon became aware that on occasion more extreme measures could be taken to deter the blackmailer. One rent boy who had presented a client with immoderate financial demands was unfortunate enough to fall through a shop window.

David's personal life at the weekends revolved around his house in Brighton, where he had built a California-style loggia complete with an indoor pool fringed by palm trees. He would leave the office on Friday afternoons accompanied by his driver of the moment, invariably a good-looking young man whose period of employment would vary between one week and six months. David threw lavish parties on a regular basis, inviting myriads of his celebrity clients and friends. Guests would gather around the white piano beside the pool and David would coax a performance out of a star or two. The resulting cabaret, provided by clients such as Shirley Bassey and Dora Bryan, outshone anything the public might have paid money for. Food and wine were in abundance and as the evening wore on bitchy squabbles would sometimes erupt amongst the gay fraternity.

By no means all the guests were gay, however, and at David's Christmas party I had one of the most embarrassing moments of my life. For some weeks I had been handling the divorce of Freddie Hancock, wife of the comedian Tony Hancock. Freddie was a particularly emotional client who found reason to telephone me several times every day. She was prone to repetition and it was not uncommon for the sixth call of the day to be virtually identical to the second. As the day progressed I would find it increasingly difficult to remain polite. Added to this tiresome routine was the fact that she insisted on approving personally every word of every letter that I wrote to her husband's solicitors, sometimes insisting on changes I did not approve of. In short, her relentless barrage of telephone calls had been making my life a misery, and when I walked into David's house with Caroline I was not best pleased to see her amongst the many guests, standing on the far side of the very large reception room.

After helping us both to drinks, I pointed out Freddie to Caroline, describing her as easily my most difficult client and saying that her constant telephone calls were making my life a misery. Within moments Freddie stormed across the room until her face was a few inches away from mine. I became uncomfortably aware that the buzz of conversation around us had stopped.

'So,' she said, spitting with rage, 'I am your most difficult client and my telephone calls are making your life a misery.' I stood in amazement as she continued: 'I'd have you know that I was brought up with a deaf and dumb child and can lip-read across a room.'

No response came to my prayer that the floor should open and swallow me up. Gradually the conversation resumed around us. To her credit, Freddie later allowed me to make amends. Before the divorce was made final, Tony Hancock died of an overdose of sleeping pills in Australia, leaving her nothing in his Will, and she retained me to file an action against his estate. In due course it was successful and she was awarded the bulk of the estate.

Divorce, libel, fraud and blackmail were the mainstay of David's business. As the entertainment connection continued to grow, particularly in the US, David formed an alliance with Marvin M. Mitchelson, a well-known attorney in Los Angeles. Mitchelson had become famous for establishing in California law a partner's right to financial support even if the couple had never been married. The principle, popularly called 'palimony', was established in a case brought against the actor Lee Marvin on behalf of the woman he had lived with for many years. To the letterhead of M. A. Jacobs and Sons was added the address of Mitchelson's office on Avenue of the Stars in Century City and as a consequence much business was referred to Mitchelson. Many Brits in the music world were now making their names in the US, especially of course the Beatles. Their manager, Brian Epstein, was a close friend and client, and David was on friendly terms with the band members, to the extent that Ringo spent part of his honeymoon at David's house in Brighton. After Epstein's death the firm handled a number of cases for the Beatles, including the notorious drugs raid by the CID on John and Yoko.

Before then, however, at the point when I had only been in the firm for some six months, a sequence of events began to unfold which were to have far-reaching and ultimately tragic consequences. None of us in the office had any inkling of what was to happen over the next few months.

In the years before I became a partner in M. A. Jacobs and Sons the firm, in common with many other solicitors, had employed a number of enquiry agents or private detectives in divorce and litigation cases. The divorce laws were very different in those times, and in order to get a divorce on the grounds of adultery it was necessary to show that the guilty party had been seen spending the night at a hotel or house with someone other than their spouse. The evidence was supplied by enquiry agents, more often than not retired police officers whose limited ambition was matched by their intelligence. It was absolutely essential to prove guilt since financial settlements were made on that basis. In effect, if both parties in the case had committed adultery but it could be proven that the wife had done so before the husband, she might receive next to nothing.

On the day in question David announced that he had found a new enquiry agent called John Merry, who was so brilliant that he put all other enquiry agents in the shade. David immediately handed over to him most of the ongoing divorce cases and Merry became an almost daily presence in the office. His reports seemed to be exemplary and highly professional, the evidence was concise and well set out. But it did occur to me that David was spending much more time than was necessary with Merry and I began to wonder what sort of an influence Merry was having on him. My suspicions that all might not be well intensified when David developed a conviction that his offices were being bugged. He confided in me that other firms had become so jealous of his success in recent months that they would do anything to learn his secrets. In fact, such was his paranoia that he even came to believe the office had been bugged by MI5. Communications between us were sometimes restricted to written notes. In order to have a conversation about clients and cases we would have to leave the office and go across the road into St James's Park. The employees could not fail to notice David's odd behaviour, and one day when he was away some senior staff members approached me to say that they thought he was heading for a breakdown from stress and overwork. They said he must take a holiday – something he had never done before. Under the pressure of serious entreaties he did agree to check into the Priory nursing home for ten days.

I had become friendly with a number of QCs whom we used regularly in litigation, in particular Joseph Jackson, a brilliant silk who was the author of the accepted textbook on divorce law. One evening after work he told me he wanted to talk privately on a serious matter. In his rooms he came straight to the point. He had represented several parties in divorce cases where John Merry had supplied evidence for the other side. In a number of these cases extreme doubt had been cast on Merry's evidence and as a friend he thought he should warn me that it might be dangerous to rely so heavily on Merry.

After David returned to work he was still heavily stressed. He was pretending he had been on holiday and to support his story had applied fake suntan to his face, but the resulting smears unfortunately made him look like an ageing queen who had turned to drink. When the moment was right I told David of my meeting with Joseph Jackson but David would have none of it. He insisted that Merry was the most brilliant agent he had ever employed and terminated the conversation.

During this time I was dealing with Freddie Hancock's divorce. Merry had submitted his usual detailed report complete with dates and places of Tony Hancock's affair with a certain actress. When Freddie saw the report she was apoplectic. She insisted she knew exactly who Tony was having an affair with and it was certainly not the actress named in Merry's report. She dismissed the whole report as a tissue of lies and took it upon herself to have Merry investigated. As luck would have it she had a close friend who was a high-ranking officer in Scotland Yard and fairly soon it was revealed that Merry had previous convictions for fraud and had been imprisoned for impersonating a solicitor.

When David was confronted with this he was devastated. His reputation had never suffered such a serious blow. Later it transpired that Merry rarely bothered to watch the suspects he was supposed to be following. Instead he preferred to stay at home writing fictitious reports which he embellished with details to make them more convincing. As a result of his conduct several important cases had to be dropped and the papers were sent to the Director of Public Prosecutions. Subsequently Merry was found guilty of perjury.

In November 1968, some time before Merry's trial, David made his usual Friday afternoon round of the office wishing everyone a nice weekend before leaving for his house in Brighton. On the Sunday morning he was discovered by his houseman hanging by the cord of his dressing gown in the garage. He had killed himself on Saturday night. His eighty-year old mother, to whom he was devoted, was staying with him at the time.

I went to the office the following day, having made a statement to the press to the effect that business would carry on as usual. This statement was carried on the front page of the *Daily Express* and most of the day was spent fielding telephone calls from our clients. Several of the gay community, including one MP, were desperate to retrieve blackmail letters which they had left in David's care in the confident expectation that their particular problem would be 'sorted'. These clients were apparently terrified that with David's suicide their personal problems would suddenly be aired in public. I had to reassure callers that they would continue to be looked after in exactly the same way they had always been.

Throughout the week messages of sympathy poured in from all over the world. One in particular caught my attention. This was from Don Arden, the rock group manager whose daughter Sharon later married Ozzie Osbourne. After expressing his sorrow at David's death he offered to deal with John Merry in his own fashion. I had been acting for Don in a number of royalty disputes with the bands he managed and had been interested to notice that he always had a baseball bat in the back of his car. Don was not known for his interest in baseball. Reluctantly I declined his offer.

It was decided that the clients of the firm be invited to contribute to a fund which would buy a Variety Club bus for sick children in David's memory. Most of the celebrities sent in a cheque. A notable exception who made no response to the invitation was Liberace, then playing to sell-out crowds in Las Vegas. His meanness was all the more remarkable because David had successfully brought a libel action against the *Daily Mirror* for suggesting that Liberace was gay – which of course he was. The damages awarded to Liberace were at the time the largest ever awarded in the English courts.

I was now, at the age of twenty-six the sole proprietor of a celebrity law firm in the West End of London with connections to one of the best-known attorneys in Los Angeles and a client list that was the envy of many other firms. The world looked very rosy.

Having inherited the practice, one of my priorities was to limit the damage arising from the false evidence presented by John Merry. Although the firm handled the usual run-of-the-mill legal business such as conveyancing, wills and probate, its speciality was litigation of every kind including libel, divorce, breach of contract and personal injury cases. In those days lawyers were not allowed to take cases on a contingency basis ('no win, no fee'). Court proceedings often attracted more publicity than the equivalent cases would today, and for a lawyer the most important thing was to be seen as a winner. I was able to achieve this by the simple expedient of going to court only when there was a very high chance of success. In all cases I made it a rule to engage the services of the top QC in any particular field. Unless counsel advised that we had a cast-iron case I would try to persuade my clients to settle out of court.

There were two exceptions to the rule: where cases were brought by individuals against either an insurance company or a newspaper. A sweet-faced client suing a nasty tabloid for libel will have the jury on her side from the start regardless of the evidence. As for insurance companies, juries look on them unfavourably on the basis that they have too much money. Besides, jury members have in the back of their mind the thought that perhaps one day they themselves might need to pursue an insurance claim through the courts.

When I first became head of the firm a number of clients went elsewhere, reluctant to entrust their affairs to someone as young and inexperienced as myself. But a fair number remained. One of these was Fanny Cradock, who with her husband Johnny was one of the first chefs to make a name on television. I handled an insurance case for Fanny which went on for a number of years, during which we became good friends. Fanny had a house in the South of France and had bought a new speedboat, which was delivered overland from the manufacturers to Port Grimaud. She and Johnny decided to have a launch ceremony for the boat. Johnny dressed up in full yachting gear sporting an admiral's cap and Fanny had a couture sailor-suit tailored for the occasion. A group of friends were gathered at the dockside drinking champagne as Fanny was piped aboard.

Fanny turned the ignition key and pressed the starter button. Immediately there was an enormous explosion and she was blown forty feet across the harbour. Johnny was still onshore drinking champagne and escaped uninjured. It transpired that due to a design fault petrol fumes had leaked into the engine compartment and these had exploded the moment the engine was started. It took many months for Fanny to recover from her injuries, as a result of which she was on medication for the rest of her life.

On her behalf I sued the insurers of the boat's manufacturers, who eventually – after several years – settled for a very substantial sum on the steps of the court. Insurers are notoriously slow payers. Backed by their enormous funds and served by teams of in-house lawyers, they can afford to prevaricate as long as possible in the hope that the claimant will cave in. In this particular case it was clear from the outset that the insurers were liable, but they refused to settle until we were at the door of the court, having gone through several years of litigation.

Fanny and I became good friends and because of my interest in food and cooking she sometimes used me as a guinea-pig for new recipes in her latest cookbook. I was a frequent guest at their house in Hertfordshire, but this was not always the pleasure that it might have been. I fancied myself as something of a gourmet and Fanny would seat me next to her at the dining table. I would be ordered to close my eyes while she popped a delicate morsel into my mouth whose origin I had to guess. More often than not it was some unusual part of an animal – often disgusting – which I was then forced to swallow. In this way I sampled such delicacies as sheep's eye, pike's brain and ram's balls. Fanny was very proud of her crayfish farm which she established in a stream which ran through the garden. After dinner it was crayfish feeding time and we were ushered into the garden carrying all the leftovers. Fanny was a strong-willed woman, not open to criticism or suggestions of any kind. She enjoyed flirting with men, but to other women she was rather brusque and cutting. With her over-made-up face and outlandish clothes she seemed not unlike a pantomime dame; my wife Caroline was terrified of her.

Another who stayed loyal to the firm was Joanna Lumley. When the *News of the World* ran an article suggesting that Joanna was sleeping her way to the top in show business and having affairs with various men of influence I sued the newspaper on her behalf. The article was completely untrue and we settled for £10,000 and a grovelling apology.

Another case with interesting ramifications which I handled was the sale of the yacht *Shemara* by Sir Bernard and Lady Docker to the property magnate Harry Hyams. The Dockers had one of the largest private yachts afloat, carrying a full crew of 29. Much of their time was spent in port in Monte Carlo. Lady Docker gained for herself some notoriety by burning the flag of Monaco at a dinner given by Prince Rainier, after which she was barred from re-entering the place. By the time Hyams signed the contract to buy Shemara the yacht was berthed in Southampton with a skeleton crew of five. For reasons known only to himself he decided not to proceed with the purchase and attempted to rescind the contract on the grounds that the yacht was not seaworthy. As she had passed A1 at Lloyds the previous year I didn't think much of his case.

In accordance with the contract an arbitration was held on board *Shemara* in Southampton, with experts for both parties measuring the thickness of the yacht's plates and testing all the moving parts. In due course the arbitrator found in favour of the Dockers and Hyams was ordered to pay for the yacht. The matter did not end there. Hyams appealed the arbitrator's decision on a point of law and took the case right up through the Court of Appeal to the House of Lords, where the Dockers were again successful. Eventually, after several years' litigation and an enormous bill for legal costs, which he had to pay, Harry Hyams completed the purchase.

With these high-profile cases behind me I became known as something of an expert on boating cases. When Sir Donald Gosling's new yacht *Silver Goose* sank in a storm in the Bay of Biscay the case was referred to me as the specialist on yachts. Actually I was nothing of the sort; it was just a question of choosing the right QC for the job. By following this strategy, and pursuing only those cases where I was advised we had an overwhelming chance of success in the courts, I maintained a

100 percent record of wins. This in turn brought in new clients and new cases.

Litigation is a game with two players, plaintiff and defendant, of whom only one can end up winning. I never ceased to be astonished how many cases went the whole way to an expensive and sometimes lengthy battle in court, at the end of which the loser was forced to pick up a huge bill for both parties.

In one vital respect litigation is very like gambling. You should only play when the odds are in your favour. My experience, in general, was that both parties were looking at the identical set of facts; both had the advice of teams of eminent lawyers; only rarely was there an important point of law in dispute, where views might differ on the correct interpretation of a statute which would need to be justified in an appeal to a higher court. Despite this, it was commonly the case that both parties were convinced they were in the right. Under such circumstances it takes a certain amount of courage to tell a client to drop the case and settle on any available terms. Besides this, lawyers also have a financial incentive to keep the taxi meter running as long as possible, when every day in court will add substantially to the fees.

2

The Framing of John Lennon

My encounter with John and Yoko was high drama. The infamous raid on their premises in 1968, and their subsequent arrest on drugs charges, was for me only a brief episode, but for them it had far-reaching consequences which were to dog their lives for many years. To understand the political impetus behind the arrest we need to remember the background. By 1967 the swinging '60s in London were at their peak. Carnaby Street led the world in fashion, the air was filled with talk of peace, love and flower power. And the most potent symbols of this mood of optimism were the Beatles.

At that time in England the possession of cannabis was an absolute offence to which there was no defence. The prosecution did not have to prove that the defendant had knowledge of the offence. Proof of possession was enough to secure a conviction. For anyone who might want to visit the United States at some later date, such a conviction could be disastrous. The authorities in the US took a very disapproving view of anyone convicted of possessing cannabis, and any non-national with a drugs conviction was automatically refused a visa.

Several prominent rock stars had already been charged with cannabis offences, including Mick Jagger and Keith Richards in 1967. They were both convicted and sentenced to prison terms before the convictions were overturned on appeal. The Stones were acknowledged as the bad boys of rock but the Beatles had a much less threatening public image. Brian Epstein, their manager, had taken great trouble to create and maintain a picture of them as wholesome clean-living lads who were an example to the youth of the world. It was he who dressed them in suits and ties and made sure that their names were kept out of the tabloid press. Epstein died of a drug overdose in August 1967, shortly before I joined M. A. Jacobs, but before then he had been a personal friend of David and a client of the firm, which dealt with a number of cases for Brian's management company, NEMS Enterprises.

Around this time it was becoming clear that the Beatles were no longer the cohesive entity they had once been. Their public image, once clean and bright, was tarnished by doubts over their dabbling in transcendental meditation and the influence apparently exerted over them by the Maharishi Mahesh Yogi. The group had given up live performances and John was keeping a greater distance from the other three. He had left his wife Cynthia to live with the Japanese artist Yoko Ono, whose speciality was a kind of 'performance art'. By 1968 John was living with Yoko at 24 Montagu Square, near London's Marble Arch, in an apartment owned by Ringo. This had previously been occupied by Jimi Hendrix who had installed an array of recording equipment.

It was during David Jacobs' absence from the office, while he was being treated in the Priory for mental illness, that the telephone call came through to the office from the Beatles' company Apple Corps. They rang at midday on 18 September 1968 asking for immediate assistance for John Lennon. As the only solicitor in the office I took the call. I was told that John and Yoko were in the apartment at 24 Montagu Square and that the police were at their front door with a search warrant demanding entry. John was reluctant to admit them until a solicitor could get to the scene to check that the search warrant was valid. He refused to open the door and, together with

Yoko, was subsequently charged with the additional offence of obstructing the police.

I had little previous experience of dealing with criminal matters, especially a drugs bust, so it was with some trepidation that I jumped in a taxi and set off for Montagu Square, about 15 minutes ride from the office. By the time I arrived the police had succeeded in forcing entry by breaking open the back door of the apartment. Although they were on the premises the search had not yet started. This was no small raid. There were half a dozen police together with an Alsatian that was trained to sniff out cannabis and other drugs.

I was let into the apartment by the front door where the police were waiting with John and Yoko for my arrival. After a few words of introduction I was shown the search warrant, which looked valid enough to me, though it was the first time I'd ever seen one. The apartment was a large one, with several rooms leading off a long corridor. I was immediately struck by the temperature generated by the banks of recording equipment, all of them switched on and giving off heat. The atmosphere was like a sauna, but with a much less pleasant smell – body odour mixed with a sweet-smelling incense. The place was in a state of disorder with clothing strewn around. Every flat surface was covered with ashtrays full of cigarette butts, empty glasses, milk bottles and old mugs of tea, some with mould growing in them. John and Yoko were standing close together dressed in black and seemed relaxed and calm. I learnt later that Yoko was several months pregnant, though that was not evident at the time.

As the search got under way John said to me, 'Don't worry, the place is clean. I was told a week ago this was coming down.' Actually it was Don Short, an entertainment journalist on the *Daily Mirror*, who had tipped him off the previous week that the police were planning a raid.

When the search started the police split up into groups and went off into different rooms in the apartment. It was therefore impossible for me to see everything they were doing. Cupboards were opened, drawers emptied and the dog was let loose to sniff around. After only a few minutes there was a triumphant shout from one of the men. In an area of the apartment where two policemen and the dog had been out of my sight the contents of a large trunk had been emptied out, containing some Indian-style clothing. One of the policemen was holding a piece of what appeared to be cannabis resin which he claimed to have found in an envelope at the bottom of the trunk. The police continued with a thorough search of every possible hiding place in the apartment and eventually produced a binoculars case which also appeared to contain some cannabis. The total amount involved was very small – less than half an ounce.

John and Yoko were duly cautioned and on my advice declined to say anything. Then the three of us were taken in police cars to Marylebone police station. To my surprise there were already a number of journalists outside the apartment when we left, no doubt tipped off by the police who must have been confident their raid would be successful.

At the police station John and Yoko were charged with possession of cannabis and obstructing the police and had to undergo the ordeal of being fingerprinted. Time was taken in detailing dates of birth and other personal particulars for the charge sheet. After an hour or more they were bailed to appear the following morning at Marylebone Magistrates Court.

Up to this time little had been said between us except to give the police the necessary details. Now that the enormity of the event was evident we had to discuss where to go from the police station. There was no question of going back to Montagu Square because word had spread, no doubt with some assistance from the police, that John and Yoko had been arrested. The press were gathering outside the police station and it was likely that even more were waiting at Montagu Square. The Apple offices in Savile Row were out, as was any address with a connection to the Beatles. We had to find a private address unknown to the press.

The easiest solution seemed to be to take them home with me. At that time we (my wife and I plus an old family nanny) lived in Redcliffe Road in Chelsea. I was confident that the press would not be able to track us down if we could get out of the police station unnoticed. I had someone from the office arrange a car and the police allowed us to leave by the rear entrance of the station. To ensure that we could reach our destination without being followed I let them think we were on our way back to Montagu Square by a circuitous route. It was evident that they were keeping the press abreast of developments.

Having spent a couple of hours at the police station, it was mid-afternoon before we reached my house. My wife Caroline was away at the time so we had the house to ourselves apart from Nanny, an old lady in her seventies.

Having managed to lose the press we settled down to pass the time before the court appearance the next morning. I had a long discussion with John about the motivation for the raid. We agreed there must have been instructions from someone high up for a search warrant for a private home to be issued. John thought he had been singled out as the most influential member of the Beatles and was certain that the Establishment were out to get him for not setting the right example to their huge fan base. He insisted that the police had planted the cannabis in the trunk at Montagu Square but was not so sure about the binoculars case.

As John had been tipped off a week earlier that a raid was imminent there had been plenty of time to get rid of anything incriminating. There was even time between the arrival of the police with the search warrant and their gaining entry for John to have disposed of any illegal substances. He was certainly sober and straight enough at the time to have made sure the place was clean and was too intelligent to have left any incriminating substance where it could be found. The fact that the press were at Montagu Square even before anything had been found caused me to have grave misgivings about the conduct of the police. I believed, as John did, that he had been set up. He referred to the copper who claimed to have found the drugs as 'a Mersey trout'. It was years before I found out that this was Liverpudlian for a turd.

We talked about the consequences of a conviction. John told me he was aware of the US visa difficulties that a conviction might bring, though he could not have foreseen the enormous problems it would create for him and the years it would take for them to be resolved. We discussed the possibility of fighting the case on the grounds that the cannabis had been planted but soon realised that this was really out of the question. There were too many police witnesses involved. In any event John was much more concerned about Yoko than he was about himself. As an alien living in the United Kingdom, Yoko would have been liable for deportation if convicted of an offence. John was resolved to admitting possessing the cannabis on the basis that Yoko knew nothing about it. However, there remained the problem of the charge of obstructing the police. As Yoko was in the apartment with John she was held equally responsible for failing to open the door to admit them.

While Yoko was in my house she seemed preoccupied with the layout of the house, insisting that the curtains must be drawn and the lights turned off, with the result that we were sitting in semi-darkness. She was also concerned about the street number. Our house was 35 and I gathered from Yoko's conversation with John that she did not consider thirty-five a propitious number. As time went by she became restless and pressed John to find another address where they could lie low.

We talked about the death of Brian Epstein a few months earlier. There had been press speculation that Brian had committed suicide, although the coroner's court had found that Brian had accidentally taken a lethal dose of sleeping pills. John was convinced that Brian would never have taken his own life. Yoko seemed distracted and didn't join in the conversation except to press John to find somewhere else to stay. John was happy to discuss any subject except the Beatles. When I asked if they would ever perform together again he didn't answer except to say that he was more interested in developing projects with Yoko than anything to do with the Beatles.

By the time evening came around we had not eaten all day. John and Yoko were hungry but wouldn't take anything I offered them except bread and jam, as they were strict vegetarians. Between us we managed to eat the best part of a loaf of bread. Although alcohol was offered, the only drinks that were accepted were cups of tea. To pass the time we played some records, but John gave no indication that he was impressed by my collection of soundtracks from *The Boyfriend* and *My Fair Lady*. A particular favourite of mine at the time was *Oh! What a Lovely War*, containing songs from World War I. The sentiments of the musical are impeccably anti-war, but unfortunately the message was lost on John and Yoko, who as total pacifists abhorred the apparent jingoism of it.

It was obvious that John was obsessed with Yoko. Whatever she suggested was acted upon. He was persuaded to telephone friends to find another place where they could go. Much later in the course of the night a car called to collect them and I said I would see them in court the following morning. The hearing was to be a formality. John and Yoko were to be released on bail to give them time to prepare their defence.

The following day the scene at the Magistrates Court was pandemonium. The arrest of a Beatle for possession of drugs was world news. The public gallery was packed and there were hundreds more in the street who could not get into the court. The press section of the court had overflowed onto the lawyers' benches. My experience of criminal court procedure was nil, having spent my years of training with an old established firm of the Dickensian variety specialising in trusts and tax. But there was little for me to do. I spoke my few words, which were to ask for bail and time to consider the charges. Bail was granted and the case was adjourned for five weeks.

My wife, who had been away for a few days, knew nothing of my involvement in the case until I got home. She had been surprised to find there was no bread in the house, and more surprised by Nanny's explanation that 'the beetles' had eaten it.

Shortly after this I was notified that John and Yoko had decided to engage a firm of lawyers who specialised in criminal law. Five weeks later John pleaded guilty to the charge of possessing cannabis and the charges against Yoko were dropped. In reality John had no choice. Had he not pleaded guilty, Yoko would have been charged with obstruction, convicted and then deported.

It was this conviction that was to cause John so much trouble in years to come. After he decided in 1971 to live permanently in New York the Nixon administration decided that his presence in the US was against the national interest and brought pressure to bear via the US immigration authorities. They refused him a visa extension and tried to have him deported on account of his conviction for possession. For five years he was unable to leave the US for fear of being refused re-entry. After numerous appeals the New York Supreme Court eventually ruled in John's favour in 1974 and the following year he received his

Green Card entitling him to residence in the US.

In February 2004 Mick Jagger, in an interview with the *Guardian*, alleged that the police planted drugs at his house in Cheyne Walk in 1969 in an attempt to frame him; a few years later senior detectives of Scotland Yard's drug squad who had been involved with Lennon's arrest were on trial at the Old Bailey for corrupt practices. Police Sergeant Norman Pilcher, who took part in the raid which resulted in Lennon's arrest, was subsequently jailed for planting drugs on an innocent victim in another case.

In September 2004 a Los Angeles Court ruled that the FBI must hand over the remaining secret files on John Lennon to Professor Jonathan Wiener at the University of California, Irvine. The US Government had argued that the release of the last ten pages would pose a national security risk because a foreign government secretly provided the information. Professor Wiener, who has waged a legal battle over the documents for more than twenty years, has yet to see them and it may be several years before the various routes of appeal available to the US Government are exhausted.

There can be little doubt that the foreign government which provided the secret information was the British Government. One can only speculate exactly what information was passed to the FBI, but it seems likely that it relates to Lennon's arrest and conviction in London for possession of cannabis in 1968. Why should the US and British governments want to keep this information secret nearly forty years after the event? Whatever still remains hidden, it is plain that there are compelling reasons to believe that the cannabis found in the apartment was planted by the police.

3

A Nice Little Earner: the Portman Agency

When I qualified as a solicitor I did not relish the prospect of spending the rest of my life in the legal profession. Rather I saw a legal qualification as a door opening onto a number of other businesses, such as property development or corporate finance. But however wide the range of possibilities I might have imagined for myself, it would certainly not have embraced the idea of owning an escort agency. Nor was this the kind of thing my careers master at Eton had in mind when he prepared his pupils to go out in the world. So I was as surprised as anyone when I became the proprietor of the Portman Escort Agency.

During the course of practising law I was often involved in property transactions for clients. One afternoon I had an appointment at the offices of an estate agent with whom I was negotiating the terms of a lease. The meeting went on for hours and, having had a few glasses of wine for lunch, I had to take a break to relieve myself. I was directed to some toilets in the basement where I noticed half a dozen very attractive girls, dressed up to the nines in evening clothes, fully made-up and looking as if they had come straight from the hairdressers. I wondered what these girls were up to in the middle of the afternoon and asked the estate agent what was going on. I was told that the basement was leased to the Portman escort agency. My curiosity got the better of me and I paid another visit to the toilet.

By the end of the afternoon I'd visited the toilet so many

times that the man behind the desk asked me if I had a prostate problem. I got into conversation with him and he told me that he was the owner of the agency and was thinking of retiring. I gave him my card and told him to call me if and when he decided to sell. I thought it might be a chance to pick up a new client. To my amazement he called the next day. It turned out there was a problem with the permitted use of the premises and he was asking for a very modest sum for the business which had been profitable for quite a few years. On an impulse I said I would buy it and we quickly struck a deal.

I was very wary of taking on a business which could be thought to be sailing close to the wind but after taking a hard look at it I was satisfied that it was perfectly legitimate. It had a valid business licence, was registered for VAT and filed tax returns and accounts at Company's House. I even took the precaution of getting an opinion from leading counsel that owning an escort agency did not leave one open to a charge of living off immoral earnings. All the same I determined to keep a low profile. Association with an escort agency might well not have been viewed as appropriate by the Law Society, whose rules all solicitors were obliged to follow.

The problem with the premises was that they were not properly designated for office use. The City of Westminster, the relevant local authority, was trying to get the agency evicted. At around the same time the government passed the Employment Agencies Act which required all agencies to be licensed and to have premises with planning permission for office use. Luckily there were some premises going in Paddington Street which had previously been occupied by an employment agency and where there was no restriction on staying open late at night. I signed up immediately and soon afterwards the Portman was issued with an employment agency licence. The framed certificate had pride of place on the office wall and the Portman was probably the only escort agency in London with a proper licence.

The key person in the agency was the receptionist, who fielded all telephone calls and dealt with any clients who called in at the agency in person. It was very important that she said the right thing to any callers. We provided a service of introduction to clients who wanted company for the afternoon or evening. What went on between the clients and escorts was none of our business. We made it very clear to any callers that we did not offer sexual services of any kind. I managed to recruit as receptionist a girl who was a pupil in barristers' chambers. In the annals of escort agencies this was perhaps a first – to be owned by a solicitor and run by a trainee barrister! There were plenty of clients who wanted to book the receptionist for escort duties but that was strictly against the rules.

The agency operated from early afternoon until late at night. During the course of the afternoon a few girls would come in looking for a booking. They hung around in their lounge drinking coffee and watching TV. When a client dropped in looking for an escort the girls would come out one by one to meet the client who would then decide which one to book. But most bookings were made over the telephone and it was up to the receptionist to choose which girls went out on any particular job. Obviously a booking to escort a client at the Park Lane Hilton was more sought after than being sent to meet a client at the Strand Palace Hotel, for example. The receptionist had a difficult job balancing jobs between the girls. It had to be borne in mind that if one girl didn't get enough of the better bookings she would leave us to join another agency.

At any given time there were thirty or more girls on our books. They came from all walks of life and were mostly pleasant and well-educated. Some were married with children and only worked afternoons. I often wondered if their husbands knew what kind of work they were doing. The younger ones were clearly in it as much for the fun of being entertained by rich clients as anything else. The names of the best dozen or so girls, the ones who were the most attractive and sophisticated of the bunch, were kept in a black book. These girls seldom came into the agency to wait for a job. They would telephone daily to say whether or not they were available for the evening.

I was amazed to see the names and photos of some of the best girls appearing in the gossip columns. One who had a lavish apartment in Eaton Square was the ex-wife of one of the richest men in London. I can only imagine that she was in it for kicks as she was certainly not short of money. Another often appeared in the pages of *Tatler* magazine and was to be seen at parties and art gallery openings on the arm of some eligible young man. Some girls operated according to a moral code of their own, which forbade them to take gifts of money from a boyfriend. This meant they needed the generous tips for escort services to keep them in designer clothes and handbags.

The Portman was promoted with a full-page advertisement on the back cover of the magazine *Where to Go in London*. The agency was constantly on the lookout for new girls as clients who came back repeatedly were often looking for new material. Ads were placed in the London evening papers for new girls offering the potential of earning a decent weekly amount and having an interesting time. When a new girl was taken on she had to sign a contract which included a declaration that she was not on the game and had never been arrested for soliciting.

I learned later that there was a strict hierarchy in the girlie business. At the bottom were the streetwalkers and common prostitutes who worked out of flats in the red light districts with illuminated doorbells going under such names as Denise Bunny; next were the hookers who could only be contacted through a madam; one more rung up the ladder were the girls who worked as hostesses in bars – possibly available for extras but more often than not simply pushing cheap bubbly as fine champagne at exorbitant prices. At the top came the girls who worked as escorts. They received a small fee from the agency, which in theory was payment for the pleasure of their company for the evening or afternoon. Any additional services for which the client might proffer a decent tip were entirely at the girls' discretion. They did not think of themselves as hookers and to have suggested that they were would have insulting.

Clients were sometimes back at the agency within minutes of leaving with a girl, presumably because they could not agree terms or perhaps the girl was not willing to perform to the client's requirements. In those cases the client would be offered another girl or a refund. Clearly there were many satisfied customers because the level of repeat business was high. I put this down to the skill of the receptionist is sending out the right girl or girls for any particular job. When an Arab prince called from a suite at the Dorchester asking for six girls for an all night-party, one can only imagine what went on. These jobs were much sought after as the Arabs were extremely generous with tips.

Although I was completely satisfied that the escort agency was perfectly legal on the basis that we only received an escort fee for the introduction and never took any money from the girls, I rarely visited the premises. I preferred to have a weekly meeting with the manager/receptionist who went through the figures and gave me the lowdown on any gossip. One might ask why, as senior partner of a law firm whose clients were often in the limelight, I would involve myself in a business which, to put it bluntly, was in the sex trade. It was not the money, which was nothing much compared to the fees earned by the law firm. I found it exciting to have an interest in a naughty, slightly dubious, agency which dealt with lovely young girls. The thought of being exposed, the field day the press would have, the horror my parents would experience if they knew, all added a kind of thrill to the boring life of being a solicitor with an Old Etonian tie. My friends thought it was hilarious and several of them were regular visitors to check out the talent on display.

Although many of the clients were foreigners, a large proportion of them coming from the Emirates, some were English visitors to London looking for a good time. The English clientele tended to go for a less attractive type of escort. Perhaps they were overwhelmed by too much glamour. In any event some of the busiest girls were not great lookers but more of the girl-next-door type. The girl most in demand was a very ordinary-looking Polish girl who went by the name of Julie. She appeared to be a sweet, gentle type and was not at all glamorous. Yet she was in constant demand from repeat customers. How she entertained her clients for the evening remains a mystery. It must have been something very special.

I did some market research at another escort agency in Chelsea. The girls were not on the premises but the client chose one to his liking from a book of photographs. I selected an escort called Miranda, who I was told was 'a posh bird', and arrangements were made for us to meet in a pub in Knightsbridge where I handed over the modest escort fee. We had an amusing dinner in a trendy restaurant and I learned that her boyfriend was a well known writer and illustrator. The problem was that as well as occasional writer's block he had perpetual erectile block. In other words he was not interested in sex. Miranda and I became good friends and I saw her several times. She never asked for anything more than the escort fee. To have taken money for sex was psychologically abhorrent to her.

Some of the escorts, no doubt, were in it for the sole purpose of extracting as much money as possible from the clients and were willing to do anything necessary to achieve their aim. On the other hand, there were plenty who did not see it as a business but viewed their activities as a series of dates during which they would get a handsome tip for pleasing their companions. There was much that was more relaxed in those far-off distant times of the '70s. The girls were nearly all home-grown; as yet there was no great influx from Russia or Eastern Europe, as travel was far more restricted and visas were hard to come by. There was no threat of AIDS, which was still unknown. The motive of many of the girls for doing what they did seemed to be not so much earning a living as having a good time at someone else's expense.

From time to time a girl would be booked for a special occasion. A peer of the realm who happened to be a good friend of mine wanted to surprise his younger brother Maurice on his 30th birthday with a lavish party which included a girl jumping out of a cake. He booked a girl from the Portman for the job. The party took place at a well-known country house hotel. The girl was smuggled into the kitchens and hidden in an elaborate cardboard confection on a trolley. During the singing of 'Happy Birthday' the trolley was wheeled in and the girl appeared out of the cake and sat on Maurice's lap. All went well, perhaps a little too well. The girl spent the night with the birthday boy, who then became smitten with her. Flowers and chocolates started arriving at the agency on a daily basis. At first the girl loved the attention but after a while, as Maurice became totally obsessed, she took fright and moved to another agency, leaving poor Maurice distraught and heartbroken.

The business more or less ran itself thanks to the efficiency of the receptionist. In general there were remarkably few problems. At one point a rival concern tried to put us out of business by blocking our phone lines. They would telephone our numbers and then leave the phone off the hook so that our lines were permanently engaged and clients could not reach us. Eventually one of the calls was traced to a massage parlour which ran ads in the same publication as our own. The situation was resolved when the massage parlour was raided by the police and closed down. With that one exception, there were no threats from rivals and no approach was ever made by anyone from the London underworld for 'insurance'.

After the agency had been running for over a year and I had got to know some of the girls by name, our receptionist, Katie (successor to the would-be barrister) suggested that we hold a Christmas party. Of all the many parties I have attended in my time I can't remember another where the girls outnumbered the boys by 10 to 1. The male contingent consisted of just me and one of my best friends. Copious amounts of champagne were downed and I found myself cornered in a bedroom with half a dozen lovely girls in advanced states of inebriation. When the girls started taking off my clothes I thought this was to be the Christmas present of a lifetime, but to my eternal disappointment all they were interested in was stripping me and then tossing me in a blanket until I touched the ceiling. So all I got for throwing the party was a sore behind when they finally dropped me on the floor.

When I decided to move to California it was time to dispose of the agency. It was bought by a plumbing company and continued trading as the Portman Agency for many years. The week before I left for the US I threw a farewell party for a dozen close friends. We warmed up at Trader Vic's with lethal rum concoctions called Samoan Fogcutters and followed those with a lavish dinner at the Mirabelle. To round off the evening I had booked a group of the best girls from the Portman to join us for the evening in a suite at the Hilton in Park Lane. After a few bottles of champagne they proceeded to entertain the assembled company with a truly memorable display which began with the girls pairing off and dancing around the suite to the sound of slow Sinatra ballads, all the time undressing each other. For what followed some of the guests were content to remain in comfort on the sofas, but others preferred to get a closer view of the proceedings by lying underneath the heavy glass-topped table in the centre of the room. Images, as one friend said to me later, that would be etched into his brain for the rest of his life. As an ex-proprietor, I allowed myself a quiet glow of pride.

4

Road Trip Misadventure

Built in the middle of the eighteenth century, 44 Berkeley Square is a magnificent example of William Kent's architecture with one of London's finest stone staircases. In the early 1960s when gambling was legalised in Great Britain it was bought by John Aspinall. Aspinall, himself a renowned gambler, was known for the private gaming parties he held in various locations all over the capital. Having fallen foul of the law on several occasions whilst operating these private chemin de fer parties, Aspinall was considerably happier than most with the change in the law.

No. 44 was to be named the Clermont Club, an exclusive members-only club where gamblers would lunch and dine in extreme comfort. The Club was a testament to Aspinall's taste and sense of style. Food and wine, both outstanding, were complimentary for the regular gambling member. Antique furniture filled every room and no expense was spared in the restoration of the house. The overall effect was that of a latter-day Regency gaming house populated by a mixture of aristocrats and rich businessmen. No. 44 also had a basement which was of no immediate use to Aspinall, but thanks to the extraordinary imagination of one of his close friends, Mark Birley, it was transformed into a nightclub which quickly became London's most elegant nightspot. This was Annabel's, named after Birley's wife.

Although the two clubs had separate entrances and operated independently many people were members of both. A small spiral staircase connected the two and during the course of the evening Mariano, Aspinall's chef de jeu, would come down into Annabel's to trawl the tables for punters. In most cases Aspinall's members, fuelled by champagne and claret, did not need much urging to join the games of chemin de fer that took place nightly. On some occasions a particularly large fish would be caught in the net and there would be much activity upstairs to make sure that the stakes were high enough. House players financed by Aspinall himself were summoned from all corners to make up the game in case there were not enough outside players; they included his own mother, Lady Osborne, known to all and sundry as Lady O.

In the mid-sixties the Clermont held its first World Back-gammon Championship. The club was invaded by an assortment of American professionals from New York and Las Vegas, together with some of their European counterparts, and though the social mix was possibly not entirely to the proprietor's taste, the level of gambling that the week of the Tournament produced more than made up for it. Certain things, however, Aspinall was not prepared to tolerate. When he heard his club described as a 'gilded pigeon-loft' by Tim Holland, one of the American backgammon pros, he banned Holland from the club for life.

I joined the Clermont Club in 1971 and became a regular blackjack player, though for modest stakes. In those days 'Lucky' Lucan was a permanent fixture at the club, before the night in 1974 when his children's nanny was found battered to death in his wife's house. Subsequently a coroner's jury named Lord Lucan as the murderer. He was given the name Lucky after winning £20,000 at Le Touquet, I was told, but from all I could see he was one of the most consistent losers at the Clermont tables. Although Lucan was invariably seated at the chemin de fer table whenever I visited the Clermont, only once did I have occasion to hold any conversation with him. Once a year the

Clermont ran a backgammon competition for its members as a two-man team event. I found myself partnered with Lucan. He asked me to lunch with him at the club in order to run through the finer points of play. I learned nothing new about back-gammon, at which I was a relative amateur, but I was intrigued to discover that Lucan ate the same lunch at the Clermont every day, week in week out, namely lamb cutlets. The only variation was seasonal; in winter they were hot (grilled) and in summer cold (*en gelée*).

Lucan was tall, with an imperious manner, and the seigneurial air extended to everything he surveyed. My order of chips to accompany grilled sole was met with a look of aristocratic disdain. On the night of the competition when it was my turn to play Lucan stood behind me, tut-tutting whenever he dis-approved of my moves. This was so unnerving that I made a basic error after throwing a double six, which should have put us in the lead. I moved to the wrong points and handed the match to our opponents. 'I thought you said you could play backgammon, old boy,' was Lucan's only comment. After this expression of his displeasure he never spoke to me again.

Like most blackjack players I had good nights and bad and never did any real damage either to myself or to the Clermont; that is, until one night in the summer of 1973 when I sat down to play in partnership with my gambling pal of the time, Jimmy Armstrong. Jimmy was an Eton-educated Australian. A com-pulsive gambler who would bet on anything, Jimmy used to spend a large part of the year in England. During the day he would be at the racecourse. In the evenings he dined in London's finest restaurants with one or other of his many girl-friends before going on to play blackjack, chemin de fer or poker at a variety of casinos. Never one to hide his feelings, Jimmy would get noisier and noisier when he was on a winning streak and sullenly silent when losing He was described by the credit manager at the Clermont as 'odious in victory, crawling in defeat'.

On that particular summer evening we were very low on cash and had run out of credit. Dan Meinertzhagen, who helped Aspinall run the casino, was a friend of mine and I managed to squeeze a last £100 out of him by telling him that Caroline was pregnant and I'd call the baby Dan if it was a boy. Since we'd already settled on the name I felt the offer was a safe one.

Jimmy and I split the £100 and sat down at the blackjack table. There followed a run of luck the like of which I had never seen before. For the next few hours we won consistently. Every time we doubled the dealer would go bust, and if one of us lost a hand the other nearly always made up for it. This was meat and drink to Jimmy. His Australian accent, normally fairly well concealed, became more strident as he started to taunt the dealers. 'Oh dear, we've lost again,' he'd say. 'You've got 22 and we've only got 21.' Dealers changed at an ever-increasing rate as the management attempted to change the run of cards but we carried on winning. Piles of £5 chips were exchanged for £100 chips and our stakes increased. Then, after playing for more than three hours, we lost three hands in a row and Jimmy stood up saying loudly, 'It's impossible to win here, the game is fixed. We're leaving.' We cashed in our mountain of chips and made for the staircase leading to Annabel's. Our original stake of £100 had increased to just over £16,000.

Jimmy ordered the best champagne and bacon and eggs and as soon as we'd finished insisted on returning upstairs for a few more hands. My instinct was to try and stop him, having known so many people who had gone back after a break to find that their luck had deserted them, with predictable results. Jimmy would have none of this defeatist talk and settled down at the blackjack table again, dragging me into the neighbouring chair. The management had mixed feelings about seeing us again.

On the one hand they were keen to recoup their losses, on the other Jimmy's appalling behaviour did nothing to endear him to the dealers, the staff or indeed any of the other punters.

To my amazement we started winning again and with Jimmy upping the stakes we added another £9,000 to our winnings within three-quarters of an hour. As soon as we lost a significant hand I hauled Jimmy to his feet and we cashed in once again. We had won just over £25,000, an amount that at that time would have bought a small house in London. This further success precipitated a final visit for the evening to Annabel's where Jimmy announced to everybody he knew that he had found his own mint and that breaking the bank would only be a matter of time. As we stood up to leave Jimmy suddenly said, 'Tell you what, Nicky, let's have a week in Cannes with the girls. You and I'll drive down. You get a car and I'll book the hotel.'

The following day found me test-driving a metallic electric blue Jensen Interceptor, one of the fastest cars around. 'I'll take it,' I said to the bemused salesman who had hardly begun on his sales pitch. He was even more bemused when I arrived later that afternoon with a bundle of cash in payment. Jimmy had already booked a large suite at the Hotel Martinez in Cannes and that evening we sat down to dinner with a copy of the Michelin guide in order to plan our itinerary.

Having taken the ferry to Dieppe we made it to Rouen for lunch. Rouen is famous for its duck dishes; also as the place where Saint Joan of Arc was burned at the stake in 1431. Our target the following day was the finest restaurant in France outside Paris, the Auberge de l'Ill near Strasbourg. But I was over-optimistic about the time it would take to reach the restaurant and we missed our reservation for lunch. While we waited for another table to become free we enjoyed a bottle of vintage champagne in the tranquil garden bordering the River

Ill. Flush with our Clermont winnings, we ordered two bottles of Chateau Mouton-Rothschild to go with the meal.

Perhaps anxious about our extravagant wine order, the co-owner and maître d'hôtel, M. Haeberlin (whose brother was the chef) personally came to our table to go through the menu. He was immaculately dressed in a morning coat and had an air of serious formality. We settled on our starters and then M. Haeberlin ran through the elaborate descriptions of the entrées. He came to truffled fillet of venison *grillé au feu de bois* – cooked on a wood-fired grill. I don't know what came over me, possibly just the effect of the champagne or something that had stuck in my mind from our visit to Rouen, but I blurted out in my schoolboy French, '*Grillé au feu de bois*, you mean like Joan of Arc. She was roasted on a wood fire.' A sharp kick in the shins from Jimmy reminded me that I had insulted the patron saint of France and the greatest heroine her country had ever known, all the more revered locally as she had been born in neighbouring Lorraine. M. Haeberlin took off his glasses and treated me to a Gallic glare. Then an extraordinary transformation took place. The glare turned slowly into a grin; he slapped the table and burst into laughter. '*Grillé comme Jeanne d'Arc*', he kept repeating as if it was the greatest joke he had ever heard. Soon he was going round the restaurant telling the story to the other diners. We became the heroes of the day. Drinks were sent over from other tables. We were asked to sign menus. After our lunch M. Haeberlin plied us with his finest Armagnac until the early evening. The next day he sent us on our way with a note addressed to his friend Paul Bocuse of Lyon, at that time the most famous chef in all of France, which read '*Soignez bien mes amis d'outremanche*' – look after my friends from across the channel. The following evening we were treated like royalty at Monsieur Bocuse's multi-starred establishment at Collonges au Mont d'Or.

It soon became clear that Fate regretted having provided such a perfect start to our holiday. But she quickly figured out the easiest way to bring us down to earth by presenting us with the sight of a casino at Aix-en-Provence. 'We'll teach these Frogs a lesson', was Jimmy's comment to me as we sat down at the tables. Because UK citizens at that time were subject to strict exchange controls, I was only allowed to bring £100 with me out of the country, and all the travellers cheques were in Jimmy's name. An hour later we were cleaned out with nothing but the cash in our pockets.

Arriving in Cannes the next day we made no mention of the casino but told the girls we'd been robbed on the way down. Jimmy's girlfriend was full of sympathy, exclaiming 'Oh, you poor guys! Were you hurt?' Caroline knew us rather better. 'So which casino was it that had the pleasure of your company?' We were forced to stay in the hotel in the evening and order from room service. Jimmy told us not to worry as he had sent a cable to his bank in Australia to wire funds to the American Express office in Cannes. The next afternoon – no word from Australia at the Amex office. Three more days and still nothing. Things were getting uncomfortable. The hotel manager was pressing for some payment on account, we were fed up with ordering from room service and, even worse, the girls had no shopping money.

On the sixth day the cashier in the Amex office smiled and beckoned us over to the counter. At last, the long-awaited telex from the Bank of New South Wales. The contents were not helpful: 'Cannot comply. B of NSW.'

'Only one answer,' said Jimmy, 'I'll fly back to London and borrow the money from my bookmaker.' The girls at least had return tickets and we pooled what little money we had left to buy a ticket for Jimmy. Before leaving he gave me some advice. 'Whatever you do, don't let the hotel think we've done a runner. Order dinner for four as usual and flush whatever you don't eat down the toilet.'

He telephoned the following day. 'Bad news, I'm afraid. My bookie wasn't at Lingfield and I can't find him until tomorrow.' I was about to keel over in despair when Jimmy added, 'Only kidding. I'll be back tonight with the dosh.' True to his word he returned with a bag full of ready cash. We settled up with the hotel immediately and hit the road. This was a very different drive from the outward journey, stopping only at petrol stations and eating only ham sandwiches. We arrived back in London completely broke and with an intense dislike of French casinos.

5

Denny Cordell and Shelter Records

To add to the clientele I had inherited in my solicitor's practice, more than a few new clients were also arriving, usually by word-of-mouth recommendation. The one who changed the course of my life, the record producer Denny Cordell, was referred to me by an old school chum, Perry Eliot, heir to the Earldom of St Germans.

Denny had established himself as a successful record producer at a very early age, a long time before we met. Though he never learned to play an instrument or read a note of music, he had an uncanny ability to tweak the mixing board in the studio until the track sounded right to him – he had 'ears', as the industry expression goes. His early hits included 'Whiter Shade Of Pale' for Procul Harum, and 'Go Now' for the Moody Blues, the latter his first attempt at making a record which went straight to number one and changed his life overnight. Previously he had been sticking stamps on envelopes for the Moody Blues' management. During this early-sixties golden age Denny recorded many artists including Georgie Fame and Joe Cocker. His assistant in the early days was the now legendary Tony Visconti, who famously says of Denny in his book that his recording technique was to 'roll a huge spliff, then just lie back and let the music flow'.

Lying back, or remaining laid back, was something Denny was always extremely good at, no matter how much those around him might be losing their heads. Visconti and Denny parted company when David Bowie came along. Tony said Yes and Denny said No, and as usual nothing could persuade him once he'd made up his mind (he was the original human mule). In desperation Visconti pressed him for his reasons. 'The c—t can't sing,' said Denny. He chose to go with Cat Stevens instead and Denny and Visconti parted ways, Visconti going with Bowie and onwards and upwards generally.

The other Tony working with Denny in those halcyon days was his lifelong friend Tony Secunda, whose antics startled even the most swinging. He it was sent out the libellous post-card of Harold Wilson and his PA Marcia Falkender, as part of his campaign to promote The Move, a great band which gave him and Denny many hits, including 'Blackberry Way' and 'Fire Brigade'. Secunda notoriously auctioned the management contract of the band in New York to the highest bidder. The band later split into ELO and Wizard.

Among various eccentricities Tony Secunda had an obsession with little people. I was meeting with Denny in London when Tony called to say it was imperative that we meet him at the Dorchester Hotel in Park Lane that afternoon. He declined to give a reason but was insistent that we go. We were sitting with him in the lobby of the hotel when a couple of midgets appeared at the reception desk. They didn't seem to be having much success with the receptionist. Within ten minutes another dozen or so midgets had come through the front door of the hotel. Secunda had put an advertisement in various theatrical publications announcing that a midget was being sought for the new James Bond film and an audition would be held at the Dorchester. At least a hundred of them turned up for this non-existent audition. The whole thing was a disgraceful hoax, and typical of Secunda's idea of fun.

If there was talent out there you could be sure Denny would find it. When he found Joe Cocker he decided to get away from the claustrophobic London scene and head for the big skies and limitless possibilities of America. After making a deal with Armit Ertigan (Atlantic Records) in New York he assembled the Grease Band around Joe, an extraordinary line-up if ever there was one: Gary Busey on drums, J. J. Cale on guitar, Leon Russell on keyboards, Rita Coolidge (among others) on backing vocals. Whatever they say about memory and the '60s, no one is ever likely to forget their performance at Woodstock, especially 'With a Little Help From My Friends'.

Together with Leon Russell, Denny founded the record label Shelter in Tulsa, Oklahoma. By the time I met Denny he had parted company with Leon and established Shelter Recording Company on Hollywood Boulevard in Los Angeles. My job was to use the legal process to chase European licensees who were slow in accounting for royalties due from distribution of the Shelter catalogue. From the moment I met Denny in London we hit it off, and on top of the business relationship we became lifelong friends. We had a common interest in horse-racing and gambling in general.

On my first visit to the US in the mid-70s Denny invited me to stay with him for a few days at his house in Malibu. It was on Escondido Beach, a relatively sparsely populated stretch of Pacific Coast Highway between Malibu Pier and Paradise Cove. Sitting on the huge deck in front of the house, sipping pina coladas and gazing at the bronze goddesses sunbathing topless on the beach below us, I realized there was a different and better world far away from the High Courts of Justice in London where I was spending my days.

Over the next couple of years I made several trips to the US, spending time both in New York and Los Angeles. England was becoming more and more depressing as the government of Harold Wilson hiked the top rate of tax up to a staggering 97.5 percent. Cars carried bumper stickers with the exhortation, 'Would the last businessman to leave the country please turn out the lights'. Denny was having some problems at Shelter Records and when he asked me if I would be interested in helping out in Los Angeles for a year or two I jumped at the opportunity. Leaving the law firm behind in 1977, I moved with my wife and two children to Brentwood, a suburb of Los Angeles between Santa Monica and Beverly Hills.

Before I started visiting California I was not aware of the existence of business management companies. In the UK many of the functions of business management tended to be spread between family solicitors, accountants and personal assistants. When I decided to give life in California a try, my first thought was to open a law office as branch of my solicitor's firm in London. I soon discovered that to do this I would be required to pass the California bar exams and I had neither the time nor inclination to go back to school. Then I was introduced to the company that was acting as business manager to Shelter Records (amongst others) and realised that this was the route to take. To be a business manager required no qualification. Denny Cordell suggested that I should become in-house business manager for Shelter Recording Company and its associated music publishing companies.

First I had to get a Green Card to enable me to work and reside in the US. As Shelter was an international business it was not difficult to convince the authorities that with my knowledge of European law and foreign languages I would not be depriving an American of a job. Unlike a personal manager I took no part in the creative decisions within the company such as the signing of new artists. These were made by Denny, who had a genius for discovering new talent. Shelter was a small independent label without the resources of the majors, but from the small number of acts signed to Shelter an extraordinarily high percentage made it to a greater or lesser degree.

Leon Russell was a world star in his day, Phoebe Snow sold several million albums, J. J. Cale has a global cult following to this day, and Tom Petty and the Heartbreakers remain super-stars and performed the half-time show at the 2008 Superbowl. All these acts were not only discovered but also produced by Denny; meaning he was responsible for the content and final sound of the albums. And when he returned to the music business after a gap of more than ten years training horses in Ireland, he signed the Cranberries to Island Records, who went on to sell tens of millions of albums.

DC (as he was known to his friends) had many more interests in life than just the music business and horse-racing. When I saw him on the deck of his house in Malibu scanning the beach with powerful binoculars I assumed he was gazing at the topless beauties sunning themselves below. I was wrong. DC was a keen ornithologist who could recognise every bird in Southern California and kept notes of his sightings. When he moved to Ireland he applied the same dedicated research to Irish birds. Animals played such an important part in his life, if he had not gone into music he said he would have liked to have been a vet. He was animated by an extraordinary desire to seek out and find the best of everything, and in doing so became something of a polymath. But whatever he decided to follow up, it had to come out of his own research and his own ideas.

Inevitably, women found him irresistible. He was a great believer in trying everything at least once. No female was ever rejected on the grounds of size, shape or colour. When we were working on Flipper's Flipper's Roller Boogie Palace he took our architect's secretary home to Malibu for the night. She was a harridan, as tall as a house and hugely overweight, of Hispanic extraction complete with moustache and flowing armpit hair. The following day I asked him 'How could you stoop so low?' In his reply he summed up his whole approach to living: 'There's a thrill in exploring the unknown. I can't say I'd do it again, but I'm glad I gave it a try.'

Playboy ran an article on sex in the office and invited readers to complete of survey of what went on in the workplace. DC completed the questionnaire, stating with perfect honesty that he had had sex with every one of the twelve female employees at Shelter Records. *Playboy* published his answers, which resulted in a stream of hate-mail and threats being directed to the office. DC felt it necessary to write to the magazine saying that one of his employees had completed and returned the survey as a joke and it was all completely untrue. It's hardly surprising that such a man would never have settled down for very long with one woman. At the time of his death he had five children from three different mothers.

His taste in motor cars was similarly broad. Though he owned a Ferrari Daytona, he rarely drove it, preferring for practical purposes to use a tiny orange Honda, whose windows were left open to the weather until weeds grew on the floor in the back. DC was so attached to the vehicle that when the engine seized up he had a new one installed at a cost that far exceeded the car's value. When the Honda eventually fell to pieces he went to the other end of the scale and bought a vintage white Cadillac convertible with huge tail fins.

The pleasures of food and wine were another of his delights. It was a simple matter for fish for sea bass in the surf on Malibu beach right in front of his house, and DC was cooking these up in blackened Cajun-style long before that particular cuisine became popular. A particular feature of that coastline during the summer is the running of the grunion, when millions of sardine-like fish swim up onto the beach to spawn at night if the conditions are right, usually at full moon and high tide. It is then illegal to net or trap the fish, but everyone is permitted to catch as many as they can with their hands and carry them off, provided no bucket or other container is used. DC became expert on the times the grunion would run and used to fill his cowboy boots with hundreds of the tiny fish in readiness for a quick fry-up in peppery oil back at the house. He would then settle down with a joint and listen to his extensive collection of early reggae.

I worked in Shelter's offices for two years until it was decided to break up the company and sell its component parts. Denny was becoming disillusioned with the record business. He was an exceptional producer and second to none when it came to finding and grooming new talent for success. But it was difficult if not impossible to remain a small independent label when the majors were circling like sharks ready to entice away any artist with huge advances as soon as a first hit record appeared on the charts. Lawsuits were expensive and the majors employed a battery of house lawyers ready to wage a war of attrition until the opposition caved in with a settlement. With an eye to the future, Denny bought an estate in County Carlow in Ireland in 1979 where he could indulge his passion for breeding and training greyhounds and racehorses.

The offices of Shelter were at the seedier end of Hollywood Boulevard in a funky tract house fronted by two enormous palm trees. Various departments run by about a dozen employees handled the many aspects of a record label including promotion, distribution, foreign licences, A & R and music publishing. Next door to the offices was a larger building which housed the recording studio. The studio was manned by two engineers, Max and Alan, both Harley bikers to whom strange substances were daily bread. They lived in the studio building and were not known to appear in daylight. Amongst their many eccentricities they had nailed a series of Big Macs to the studio wall, each with a date recorded beneath. The object was to demonstrate that the burgers were so full of preservatives that they would last forever. After six months or so they became fossil-like and hard as cement. The studio window backed onto a paved yard and for some years it had been the custom to clear the studio of empty bottles by throwing them out of the window. The mountain of broken glass reached up to the level of the second floor. In spite of their alarming appearance Max and Alan were endearing characters and brilliant engineers who maintained the constant high quality of the Shelter sound.

When I arrived on the scene Shelter had a long-term contract with Tom Petty and the Heartbreakers who had broken into the big time with the release of their first two albums. A new album was in the works when a shark appeared waving a million dollar cheque if Petty would jump ship. With the help of a cunning and devious legal manoeuvre Petty moved his residence out of Los Angeles county to a different county which had more favourable insolvency laws. He was able to terminate his contract with Shelter by declaring bankruptcy and immediately afterwards became a millionaire by signing with the major label. This proved to be the last straw for Denny and he resolved to move to Ireland. My job became one of winding down the label and selling off its assets to the highest bidder. The worst task which Denny left to me was to inform the loyal Shelter employees that the label was closing and they were out of their jobs.

Although Shelter's days were numbered there were still good times to be had in Los Angeles. Before the Petty debacle Denny threw a birthday party for him in the private room of Le Dome, our favourite restaurant. Matters got completely out of control when the assembled company raced down the centre of the long dining table reducing all the glass and china to rubble.

It was at this party that I renewed my acquaintance with Don Arden, for whom I had done some legal work in London.

Don had launched a hugely successful label, Jet Records, with the Electric Light Orchestra and Black Sabbath. His daughter Sharon was dating Sabbath's lead singer Ozzie Osbourne. Don arrived at the party in his sheriff's uniform complete with 10-gallon hat and toting a gun. I remember him complaining to me that while Ozzie was a guest in Don's house he had the unnerving habit of sleepwalking into Don's bedroom and urinating on his bed.

Don asked me to visit him at his house to discuss a problem he was having with A & M records. One of the label's founders, Jerry Moss, was a close friend of Denny's and Don thought I might be able to put in a favourable word for him. Don's house was a hilltop fortress in Beverly Hills complete with barbed wire perimeter fence, guard dogs and security men with guns. I sat down to discuss the problem. Don complained that although he was having a serious dispute with A & M over distribution rights, they had had the nerve to send him a Christmas card. The Christmas card was a photograph of the founders Herb Alpert and Jerry Moss with a seasonal greeting. Don recounted his reaction: 'I was so furious I wiped my arse with the card, put it in an envelope and sent it back to A & M addressed to Alpert and Moss – two pieces of shit.' This convinced me that on no account should I get involved with any of Don's business affairs.

Waiting for the law to resolve disputes is a slow business. During the run-down of Shelter's music publishing catalogue, I was to have immediate experience of much simpler and more direct methods. Denny Cordell had been one of the first producers to recognise the potential of reggae. He brought Bob Marley from Jamaica to the US for the first time and had dealings with a number of other reggae stars. He was so taken with their music that his personalised numberplate on his Ferrari Daytona in California read 'RAAAAAS'. The Shelter catalogue included some Peter Tosh compositions, on which we were still collecting royalties. One day two Jamaican heavies pushed into my office, where I was alone at the time, and started waving a magnum 45 handgun in my face. They ordered me to stand on a chair, threatening to blow my head off if I didn't hand over all the royalties we had collected on the Tosh songs. They claimed to be the legal owners of the copyrights.

The offer of a large spliff calmed them down slightly, and I had reason to be grateful to Denny for leaving a stash in my office on an earlier trip. The problem was a simple one. Tosh, like several other Jamaican artists in the early days, was happy to take advances from several publishing companies for the rights to the same songs. These two heavies were trying to collect on behalf of another claimant to the Tosh songs. I showed them that Denny's agreement went right back to the time when the songs were first released on records, and after a good smoke and a few stiff drinks they went on their way. Sadly, the Tosh situation became such a mess that he was murdered in Jamaica a few years later.

The component parts of Shelter's catalogue were gradually sold off to the highest bidders. The most valuable item was the seven albums that J. J. Cale had recorded for Shelter. Polygram was the obvious buyer as it had signed a new deal with Cale. After some to-ing and fro-ing Polygram offered £1 million, a substantial sum in 1982. I bet Denny we could get a lot more. Using the old good guy/bad guy ploy Denny told Polygram that he thought they were being very fair but his business manager would not accept the offer. Eventually I got them up to £2 million and collected a sizeable winning wager from Denny. We went to Polygram's HQ in Holland for a signing and photo session and to collect the cheque, then headed for Paris to celebrate. Having settled into a suite at the lavish Hôtel de Crillon, I asked Denny how long we would be staying in Paris. 'Till we've spent the two million, of course' was his reply.

Today any aspiring artist can make a recording on inexpensive computer equipment in his or her own bedroom. Within minutes it can be posted on the internet where anyone in the world can listen to and download it. Even established artists now commonly release new albums on the internet. Previously, it was the record labels that held the keys to success in the music business. It was impossible for an artist to get anywhere without being signed to a label. At Shelter Records each morning, a handful of tapes would tumble through the letterbox. The unknown hopefuls who had recorded them would also have sent the tapes to dozens of other labels. Up and down the country unknown bands were playing in tiny clubs for peanuts in the hope that a talent scout would be in the audience. The record companies contained whole departments whose job it was to seek out new talent.

The gamble taken by the label in signing a new act was huge. First the record has to be cut in the recording studio. Often this takes months of expensive studio time involving engineers, producers and the living expenses of the band, many of whom need plentiful supplies of alcohol and other substances before they can perform. Even when the album is mixed, equalised, pressed and distributed no one will buy it without radio play, so thousand of radio stations across the country are sent demo tracks from the album and ads are placed in the trade press such as *Billboard*. If the album takes off the band will be sent off on a promotional tour playing in clubs and giving interviews on local radio. All of this costs the label a great deal of money. If they are lucky perhaps one new act in ten will make it on a sufficient scale to recoup the costs. Only a tiny percentage will do well enough to justify the cost of a second album. Of course, one big winner that sells millions of albums will pay for the many that fall by the wayside.

The music business was not one for faint hearts. It took the spirit of a gambler like Denny Cordell to set up his own record label when a safe position beckoned as a producer working for one of the majors.

6

Flipper's Roller Boogie Palace

On the East Coast of the US in the late '70s a new phenomenon could be seen in city parks and on the sidewalks. People were taking to roller skates as never before. Almost everyone had used them as children but what was new was the number of adults who had rediscovered the joys of skating. This was partly due to improved technology, which gave roller skates wheels and bearings borrowed from skateboards. At the Empire Rollerdrome in Brooklyn skating had been taken to a higher level with the birth of roller disco. To the same music that was being played nightly in Studio 54 and other disco temples elaborate dance routines were being performed on skates. One of the first to spot the potential of this new craze was an ebullient English friend of DC, Ian Ross, one of the founders of the pirate radio station Radio Caroline. He had once been injured in a car accident and was left with one foot that had the appearance of a seal's flipper. His pals had used this name for him ever since.

I was still in Hollywood at the time working with Denny at Shelter Records, and when Flipper reported confidently that roller disco was about to sweep the world we flew to New York to check out the skating scene.

The Empire in Brooklyn had seen better days and was in dire need of a lick of paint but the scene on the skating rink took our breath away. A great mass of skaters young and old were bipping and bopping their way around the rink in a kind of rhythmic frenzy to the discs spun by the resident DJ who had replaced the ancient Wurlitzer jukebox. After a couple of beers I said we must give it a go. Game though he was, Flipper couldn't find a rental skate to accommodate his foot, and Denny had an unshakeable aversion to any form of skating or skiing. So it was left to me to take to the floor. I had once spent many hours at an ice-rink belonging to the father of a school friend, so I didn't find it strange and soon fell into a groove. It was like being caught up in a current of swaying bodies propelled by some new energy. If anyone made a slip a dozen hands reached out to rescue the faller without any break in the rhythm.

The experience was truly exhilarating, but better was to come. At a certain point the skating floor was cleared of the general public to make way for the nightly performance of synchronised skating put on by the Roller Rocker Showstoppers. The Roller Rockers were all black and most of the time acted as skateguards for the general public. Their movement, rhythm and speed were hypnotic as they circled the roller rink, all the time dancing to the disco music being spun by the DJ, one Dr Love. The rink was in a poor area in the centre of Brooklyn, the audience was largely African-American, and the amount of money being spent was comparatively small. We decided that moving the show to an up-market venue in Los Angeles would be like taking an out-of-town musical to Broadway.

We returned the next day to talk to Dr Love. Denny asked how he felt about bringing the show to the bright lights of Tinsel Town. 'Sounds cool, but only if all twelve of my boys come with me,' was the reply. So we worked out a deal for him and the Showstoppers to come to LA as soon as we could find a suitable venue and a place to accommodate them.

For many years there had stood in West Hollywood a huge windowless building with a domed roof. It was situated at the intersection of two major boulevards, Santa Monica and La Cienega, and covered almost an entire city block. This vast structure housed Art Linkletter's tenpin bowl, with 28 bowling lanes made of the finest maple. As the popularity of bowling declined in the late 1970s the building had been put on the market. We decided this was the ideal location for our roller disco and as the business manager I started negotiations with the realtor handling the sale. The building was considered something of a white elephant, and as the only interested party we were able to strike a deal to buy it outright for around one million dollars.

I had assumed that it wouldn't be difficult get a commercial mortgage for at least half the cost – wrongly, as it turned out. No mortgage lender would believe that roller disco could be successful enough to pay the rent on the building. Luckily one of Denny's friends in the music business introduced me to Berry Gordy, founder of Motown Records, who was interested in buying real estate in Los Angeles. In return for a share in the property he put up most of the purchase price, while Denny agreed to finance the fitting out of the building. This became the world's first purpose-built roller disco. The design had elements of nightclub, theatre, bar and disco as well as the necessary roller-rink complete with skate hire and pro-shop.

The budget for fitting-out was originally a couple of hundred thousand dollars but Denny soon got carried away until the cost trebled. By opening day we were so short of cash to pay the team of craftsmen who were working round the clock to open on time that Denny had to sell his prized Ferrari Daytona convertible for quarter of a million dollars.

The 28 bowling lanes were torn up and the maple used to build banks of theatre-style private boxes around an ice-blue skating rink. With high side walls and low lighting, the boxes were perfect for carrying on any tryst or other questionable activity in almost complete privacy. The rental skates were specially made in blue suede. Students from the Los Angeles

College of Art laboured for weeks to decorate the walls with Henri Rousseau-style jungle scenes and a 40-foot high painting of Carmen Miranda which dominated an end wall. In the centre of the rink was an island stage where a fifteen-piece band played salsa music. A long bar served exotic cocktails with a Brazilian theme, including an Ipanema special which, if the barmen knew you well enough, would have a little packet of white powder taped to the bottom of the glass.

We had decided to open Flipper's as a private club. Membership was priced at $400 a year, with the proviso that anyone joining before opening day paid only $200. The day before opening there was a queue around the block. We opened with over 1000 members, and the demand for invitations to the official opening was so great it had to be spread over three nights.

One of my jobs as business manager was to ensure that we were granted the numerous licences necessary to open Flipper's Roller Boogie Palace, including permits from health and safety, the fire department, the building authority and of course a liquor licence. One might question why the authorities would even consider allowing the installation of a fully licensed bar inside a roller rink. It was all down to connections. The local politics of the day played an important role in the field of entertainment. Ronnie Reagan was in the White House and influence from Hollywood was at its zenith.

I had been introduced to an attorney of the old school, Greg Bautzer, by Ken Hyman, producer of *The Dirty Dozen* among many other movies. Greg grew up in Los Angeles with Ronnie Reagan and worked on the campaign which elected Reagan governor of California. Greg was a distinguished figure who dressed in smart suits, wore striped shirts with stiff white collars and had afternoon tea served by an English butler in his penthouse office in Century City. Whenever it looked like hurdles were being put in our way by the various licensing authorities, a call to Greg would clear the problem. His influence and contacts were far-reaching and included the chairman of the planning authority, the liquor licence bureau, the coastal commission and the city business licence office.

Flipper's duly opened on 4 July 1979. In order to add an aristocratic British flavour to the opening the invitations had been sent out in the name of Lord Peregrine Eliot, the Earl of St Germans, an old friend from schooldays who agreed to perform the opening ceremony. Publicity for the event was worked up to fever pitch by Rogers & Cowan, the top PR company in the US. The event was covered on coast-to-coast network TV. Every available searchlight in LA was hired for the event so the building could be seen for miles around. Security was provided by six enormous black pro-footballers dressed in white tie and tails.

There were a few incidents. Some celebrities turned up without invitations. One of them, George Hamilton IV, wrestled with the security guard when I said I had never heard of him and denied him entrance. The publicity generated by the skirmish only added to frenzy for membership. The top of the safe in the manager's office became the surface of choice for those wishing to indulge in a little white powder. On the advice of Rogers & Cowan a number of celebrities were given free charter membership. One of these was Dudley Moore, who sent me this unusual letter from his address in Venice Beach:

> Dear C—t,
> Thank you for the c—ting membership to your c—ting club.
> C—t, c—t, c—t, c—t, c—t, c—t, c—t, and c—t.
> Your c—ting friend,
> Dud C—t.

Dud did come down to Flipper's a few times but was never persuaded to put skates on.

Flipper's was an overnight success and became the in place to be seen. It was filled nightly with LA's most glamorous crowd of all generations who queued round the block to get in. Some came just for the spectacle and to watch the nightly performance of the Roller Rockers. Cher was there almost every night dressed in satin shorts, so much so that the press often wrote as if she were the owner of Flipper's. Sometimes she was with Olivia Newton-John, who went on to star in the film *Xanadu*, which was loosely based on Flipper's. Robin Williams, Jamie Lee Curtis and Harry Dean Stanton were regulars. Shiny spandex outfits in psychedelic shades of pink, green and turquoise were all the rage, and the roller disco exuded an exhilarating air of success and excitement. It felt more like New York and London than laid-back LA – a sort of Studio 54 meets Tramp on wheels. The place became a popular venue for TV and film locations. The Jerry Lewis annual telethon was broadcast from the roller rink.

Each night of the week had a different theme. Monday was a very popular gay night, Wednesday was New Wave, Thursday for live bands and so on. One of the first artists to play at Flipper's was Prince. When I saw him rehearsing I said to the girl who booked the talent, 'You must be joking. This guy in fishnet tights and a raincoat is never going to make it.' Later I understood how the record company who rejected the Beatles must have felt. We used any excuse to throw a party – Valentine's day, the Queen's birthday, Halloween, and Flipper's birthday when, in his usual genial fashion, he had to be restrained from offering free drinks to all comers. Daytimes were busy. We formed a Junior Roller Disco Club, with special birthday party packages including a booth, skates, a hotdog and coke and a balloon. The venue was also popular with magazines for fashion photoshoots.

Drinks were delivered to private boxes by waitresses on roller skates. To recruit the dozen girls we needed to work as skatresses we placed an ad in the *Los Angeles Times*. Two hundred applicants turned up for the audition, mainly resting actresses, and choosing the best of them was a pleasant duty. They had to negotiate several stairs to get up to the boxes, no easy task on skates while balancing a tray of cocktails. The private boxes were in great demand for obvious reasons. Bearing in mind that we never knew if there was an undercover agent from the Narcotics Bureau or Alcohol Beverage Control on the premises I urged the staff to take extreme care when examining the ID of young people. It was illegal to serve alcohol to under-21s and the penalty was loss of our licence. As fake ID was easy to obtain on the streets of LA, keeping control was not easy especially on busy nights with a thousand or more customers buying drinks.

Like many things in LA, the fame of Flipper's was short-lived. After about a year its popularity began to wane. Some members were not interested in renewing for the second year. Problems arose, not the least of which was the spate of accidents and broken limbs. Every time a fall resulted in a broken wrist or worse, the Los Angeles paramedics turned up in force with sirens blaring and a totally unnecessary fire truck in attendance. A journalist commented that he had never seen so many ambulances outside a club. Although all skaters had to sign a disclaimer on entry which absolved Flipper's from responsibility, the litigious LA attorneys had a field day. We were soon buried in an avalanche of lawsuits from Beverly Hills dentists with broken wrists claiming massive loss of earnings on the basis that it was unsafe to combine roller-skating with a full bar. Our insurance was cancelled at an early date and our attorney was fielding dozens of lawsuits.

It became increasingly difficult to fill the club with special events. Halloween was great but that was only once a year. Cash flow became a problem and we fell behind with the rent owing to Berry Gordy. Luckily help came from a most improbable source.

In my early days in London I had become an expert blackjack player through many hours at the tables in the Clermont Club. One week when it looked like we would not have enough cash to meet payroll I took the $5000 we had in hand to Las Vegas and spent the night at the Tropicana casino. With very careful play and selecting only those tables which seemed to be running against the bank I managed to double my money and the day was saved. I did even better some weeks later when after a very heavy birthday dinner with Kiefer Sutherland and his girlfriend involving many flagons of wine, Kiefer suggested we fly to Vegas. It was 2 a.m. but no matter, a limo arrived at the restaurant and took us to Burbank airport where Kiefer had chartered a jet. We were met on the runway by the MGM limo and were soon sitting at a blackjack table.

In those days Kiefer was a regular player with a large line of credit. He asked for $100,000, put half in front of me and said 'We'll play together'. This level of play was seriously out of my league. Luckily I was so anaesthetised by the wine that I didn't get up there and then and walk away. After about 10 minutes I noticed to my horror than Kiefer had reduced his pile to nothing. The dealer had enjoyed a run of luck and my pile of chips was down to half. The next 20 minutes went by in a haze. To my amazement Kiefer suddenly said, 'We're enough in front. Let's cash in now'. The total in front of me was $185,000 but I hadn't realised it. In my drunken stupor I'd mistaken the $5000 chips for $500s.

'Man, you were so cool playing $11,000 a hand and doubling up,' Kiefer said to me. I'd been staking a minimum of $22,000 per hand with an occasional double to $44,000 or more. I didn't admit that I'd thought I was playing $2000 per hand. But the result was we paid for the jet and got back to LA with $40,000 cash each in our pockets.

Our attorney stalled the lawsuits for nearly two years but there came a time when we decided to close. Roller disco had run its course. One empty Tuesday night I remember the three of us, Flipper, Denny and myself, leaning disconsolately on the rail that surrounded the skating rink.

'What's the difference between Flipper's and the *Titanic*?' I asked. There was no answer.

'When the *Titanic* went down she was full and the band was playing.'

Still, we hadn't done too badly. A year after Flipper's closed we sold the building for double what we'd paid for it. Berry Gordy was satisfied and Denny more than recouped his outlay. As for Flipper and myself, we'd spent a couple of years having the time of our lives.

7

'Good Morning, Mr President'

After Flipper's closed I moved to New York. I rented an apartment in a converted townhouse on the corner of East 62nd St and Lexington Avenue, opposite the street from Brooke Shields, who was often to be seen tending a collection of teddy bears which she had lined up on her windowsill. These were busy times and I was employing two assistants. As well as disposing of the Shelter catalogue I was now developing a new career as business manager, and one of my first assignments was to take over Ronnie Wood's business affairs and make a start on cleaning up the mess that his finances were in. Other clients were soon on the books.

My neighbour across the landing was an English aristocrat whose family owned part of the Macmillan publishing empire. He was blessed with a manner so arrogant that it would certainly have cost him his life, or at the very least serious injury, if I had not been around to rescue him. The street level of our building was occupied by a Japanese restaurant. Every night after the restaurant closed the rubbish was put on the street for collection by the garbage truck. Being Japanese, the staff took meticulous care to leave the rubbish neatly stacked outside the restaurant in orderly piles, tying any papers up with string. One night my neighbour was strolling home from dinner and as he passed the restaurant he casually threw a few pages from his copy of *The Times* onto the immaculately stacked trash. Unluckily for him at that moment the Japanese proprietor came outside.

'You pick up paper,' he said to my neighbour.

'Don't be absurd. It's garbage,' he replied.

'*Pick up paper.*' This time it was said in a loud voice full of menace. My neighbour, ignoring the man who by then was joined by the chef brandishing a meat cleaver, walked on and turned to open the street door to the apartments. Just as the two Japanese launched themselves at him screaming 'Pick up paper or we kill you,' I was on my way out of the building and had opened the inner door to the small lobby. My neighbour was halfway into the lobby as what seemed like the entire staff of the restaurant tried to grab him. I managed to drag him to the lobby side of the street door before slamming it in the face of his pursuers. To give him his due he did thank me for saving his life.

Denny was immersed in the horse business in Ireland but whenever he got a break he would stay with me in New York for a few days. His former protégé Joe Cocker was enjoying a successful world tour in spite of some well-publicised problems related to alcohol. We caught up with him one afternoon in the Mayflower Hotel in New York. Up in his suite Joe asked what we would like to drink. Knowing we had a long afternoon and ever longer evening ahead, we settled for tea. Joe called room service and placed an order in his broad Sheffield accent: 'Ah want tea for three and a bottle of rum. Ah've been here a week and can't get a proper cup of tea. Don't give me that piss-weak brown water they call tea over 'ere – Ah want some proper fookin tea with fifty fookin tea bags.' After half an hour, no sign of room service. Joe gets the manager on the phone. 'Where's mah tea with fifty fookin tea bags? And don't forget the bottle of rum. And while you're at it send up a couple of dirty girls.' Again nothing for a while, then a rattling in the corridor and a knock on the door of the suite. Four waiters appear, each pushing a trolley. On the first trolley is an enormous ornate samovar belching steam, closely followed by three trolleys laden with cups and saucers plus a bottle of rum. Joe's order has been translated as tea for fifty. Of the girls there is no sign.

Later that evening we went over to Gino's for dinner. Gino's on Lexington was my local and was frequented by many English ex-pats of the suit-and-tie variety who were not accustomed to the presence of a noisy old rocker like Joe. He was on flying form having dealt with the bottle of rum. As we were being shown to our table he stopped to have a word with an elderly gentleman dining with his wife. The man had very prominent ears whose size was accentuated by his lack of hair.

'Tell me, luv,' said Joe, 'What do you do with them ears at night? Do you fold 'em over before you go to sleep?' The poor man was too taken aback to reply before Joe moved on. A few more stops on the way to our table and Joe had the entire restaurant staring at us. Before we sat down he announced in his inimitable arm-waving fashion 'I'm Joe Cocker – star', to the surprise of the clientele. We got through our first course without incident. Then, without warning, Joe leant back in his chair and turned to a group of elderly ladies having dinner at the next table. 'Hello, luvs. Is it true girls have wet dreams too?' The question was met with stony silence until we were shown the door by the maître d'. It was some time before I dared show my face again in Gino's.

As the popularity of Flipper's Roller Boogie Palace began to wane, Ian Ross (aka Flipper) came across a business opportunity that was to take us to the desk where the buck stops, in the Oval Office of the White House. Its occupier at the time was Ronald Reagan, and the whole episode provided a small revelation of the machinations of lobbying in US politics.

Ian's father was an entrepreneur and engineer in the UK who had spent many years working jointly on projects with

Hughes Aircraft Corporation. Howard Hughes had taken a personal interest in the design of a revolutionary type of helicopter that would cost no more than a car both to buy and run and thereby revolutionise the whole concept of both global and local transportation. In consequence Jon Boseker, the chief engineer of Hughes Aircraft Corporation, had been despatched to stay with the Ross family in England to work on the project. Jon was one of the very few people that Howard Hughes trusted. After Hughes' death Jon became the curator of the Spruce Goose, the plane with the largest wingspan in the world, which was hidden away from the public in a hangar at Long Beach. Jon was also one of the few people who had access to the 9th floor of Hughes Aircraft Corporation's building at Los Angeles airport, where satellite technology was being developed and other highly secret work was carried on for the US Department of Defense.

Jon had retired to Los Angeles and when Ian looked him up he arranged for us to have a private tour of the Spruce Goose. This was a vast seaplane built of wood, which had only ever flown once, with Howard Hughes at the controls. During the course of this visit Jon mentioned that the US Government was inviting companies to apply for licences for direct broadcast satellite television, a revolutionary concept at the time. Jon also made us aware that Hughes were in the process of developing a satellite system considerably more powerful, and also less expensive, than those that had been launched previously. Ian, who was more of a visionary than a businessman, convinced me that we should apply for one of the ten licences that were to be issued by the Federal Communications Commission (FCC).

In his usual expansive manner Ian outlined how we would become the leading television network in the US. Essential to this vision was a picture of himself interviewing stars poolside in their Beverly Hills homes with a live feed to the satellite and the world. The greeter of Flipper's, writ large as well as a potential billionaire! Jon explained that the technology involved placing three or four satellites in geo-stationary orbit so that the signal footprint would cover the entire US from Hawaii to Puerto Rico. Without the slightest idea how we would raise the huge amount of funding required for the project, we decided to go for it and gave ourselves the grand name of Direct Broadcast Satellite Trust.

I found an investor who, swayed by Ian's oratory about the millions to be made, was willing to put up the money for specialist FCC attorneys in Washington to draft our application. We learned that the other applicants were the giants of the entertainment industry including CBS, NBC, MCA Universal, National Christian Network and so on. These companies all had the resources to provide television programmes 24 hours a day. We were comparative minnows but we did have the advantage of an inside route to Hughes' latest satellite technology, and their agreement to provide us with plans for a dedicated system that would be revolutionary, particularly in terms of cost, compared to anybody else's. Jon arranged for us to take the guided tour of the 9th floor and the satellite production line. There we met a young Indian scientist who worked with us. Although most of it was completely over our heads, one of his solutions was blindingly simple. This concerned the signal strength. Until then the orthodoxy was to boost it from the downlink before it returned to earth, but by the simple expedient of a chip in the uplink our guy was able to achieve the same result at a fraction of the cost.

Each satellite would cost a mere $50 million, plus launch. Plus quite a lot of other things, actually. All we needed was a few hundred million dollars to build and launch our satellites. Ian said, 'Once we have the licence from the FCC we'll be knocked over by the rush of investors pouring their millions into our coffers.' In fact we only had to find half the money as half the cost of the whole system was being met by COMSAT, a US Government-funded organisation. With more imagination than substance to our story we put ourselves forward as an entertainment group with many connections in the movie business which could deliver original programming for our channel. I made several trips to Washington to confer with FCC attorneys and work on the drafting of our application. Finally it was completed and filed with the FCC.

It wasn't long before our attorney in Washington told us that the FCC had indicated that there were several better-funded, more experienced and better-equipped candidates for the handful of potential licences. Furthermore the FCC suspected that we were 'straw men' fronting for Hughes, who under anti-trust laws could not be broadcasters. At the time the mystique and paranoia surrounding anything to do with Howard Hughes was such that almost anything was believable, up to and including the idea that he might be directing operations from beyond the grave. It was a bitter irony, therefore, that our one great advantage over our competitors should turn out to be unhelpful to our application. There was one further problem, in that FCC policy laid down that any broadcaster must be in the hands of US citizens. Issuing broadcasting licences to aliens like Ian and myself was considered to create a propaganda risk. All in all, our attorney made it very clear that our group had no chance of being granted a licence.

I had to break the news to our investor that it seemed he had lost his money. We had no idea how to get back on track until I mentioned the situation to a friend of mine, Ken Hyman, who had produced the movie *The Dirty Dozen* among many others. Ken was well connected with the old Hollywood studios, as at one time his father Elliott Hyman, a Hollywood legend comparable with Thalberg, had taken over Warner Bros and created Warner Seven Arts. Ken suggested that I should meet Greg Bautzer, an attorney of the old school who had close ties to President Reagan. Ken also agreed to become Chairman of our group, which solved the problem of US citizenship.

From the north-west corner of the penthouse office in the tallest building in Century City the eye travels down Avenue of the Stars along Santa Monica Boulevard to Rodeo Drive and on up to the Beverly Hills Hotel. This was the route taken most evenings by the occupant of these sumptuous offices on his way to cocktails at the Polo Lounge. Gregson Bautzer, senior partner of Wyman, Bautzer, Christiansen, Kuchel and Silbert was in his younger days Howard Hughes' personal attorney and represented him in his sale of Trans World Airlines. His many affairs with film stars included Lana Turner, Joan Crawford, Ginger Rogers and, more importantly to this story, Jane Wyman, who had been married to Ronnie Reagan. Greg was born in the same year as the President and was a close personal friend who had helped him gain the governorship of California.

Having met a good number of entertainment business attorneys in my few years in Los Angeles I had got used to the casually dressed, feet-on-the-desk types who were as likely to offer a line of coke as a cup of coffee. I was pleasantly surprised to meet an attorney who not only wore a stiff white collar, blue shirt and tie but was also immaculately attired in a Savile Row suit. Tall, elegant and with clear blue eyes and silver hair, the seventy-something-year-old Mr Bautzer greeted me in his Century City eyrie as his formally dressed butler served Earl Grey tea in English bone china. I too had arrived dressed in a dark suit and wearing a tie. My appearance and English accent put Mr Bautzer in a receptive frame of mind. After I outlined the situation to him he expressed the opinion that he might be able to help and suggested I meet him for a drink a few days later in the Polo Lounge at the Beverly Hills Hotel. 'Perhaps I may don my rusty armour and take up my trusty lance once more!' he rather poetically declared. I only hoped he was not going to play the part of Don Quixote.

The inner sanctum at the Polo Lounge is guarded by an officious maître d' who steers to the outermost tables in the room anyone not recognised as a mover and shaker in the entertainment world. At the mentioned of Mr Bautzer's name I was escorted to the top table where he was enjoying a cocktail with Ted Turner, the legendary founder of CNN. Both were dressed in tuxedos for an awards ceremony evening and were clearly no longer on their first drink. Risqué jokes, raucous laughter and more drinks were the order of the day.

Greg Bautzer was more than optimistic that he could be of help to our group's application for a licence and I assumed, wrongly as it turned out, that Ted Turner would in some way be involved. A day or two later I went back to Bautzer's office where he explained that the fee for his services would be $50,000 and that he would like to have it in cash. He was quietly confident that he could swing things our way. Our investor had already spent a similar sum with the attorneys in Washington which had got us nowhere, but I was able to persuade him to put up the required fee. This was duly delivered in a brown paper bag to Mr Bautzer at the Polo Lounge, again carousing with Ted Turner.

For a week or so I heard nothing more. Then I was called by his very English secretary and asked to come to his office the next day at 8 a.m., an unusually early hour for Los Angeles. I was told it was important not to be late. At the appointed hour we met. The butler was on hand to serve English breakfast tea brewed in a Crown Derby teapot in proper style. After fifteen minutes of small talk Mr Bautzer's secretary came into his office and announced that the White House was on the line.

'Good morning, Mr President – how are you?' Bautzer's voice carried a tone of many years' familiarity with his interlocutor.

'My congratulations on your administration's initiative with Direct Broadcast Satellite TV, which should bring a huge demand for new programming of which our State will be the prime beneficiary. It will be a welcome boost for the entertainment industry in Los Angeles.' After some more words in that vein, Mr Bautzer continued: 'One of my clients is having a problem with an application for a licence. My client is a group of young Englishmen living in Los Angeles who are energetic and full of new ideas and will bring a new dimension to TV programming. Their chairman is our old friend Ellie Hyman's son Ken. One of their ideas which appeals to me and I know will appeal to you is to make plenty of new movies as well as show plenty of old ones. Especially yours, Mr President!'

I realised that this conversation, though short, had been set up in advance with a Presidential aide for my benefit. If it was meant to impress it succeeded. Bautzer shook my hand and told me not to worry.

Not many days later our attorneys in Washington were surprised to hear from the FCC that, contrary to the earlier communications, our licence application would receive favourable consideration. In due course the licence was issued to our group along with those to NBC, CBS and a handful of other heavy hitters. We were deluged with enquiries from the press, who wanted to know all about Direct Broadcast Satellite Trust. We took on the role of minor celebrities again.

I met Greg for a celebratory drink in the Polo Lounge. As a joke I asked him if any part of the cash fee was going to the

President's re-election fund. Greg roared with laughter, 'Good heavens, no! I wanted the fee in cash because I like young girls'. As he was well into his seventies I hoped I would feel the same when I was his age.

Part of our plan was to make dedicated original movies under Ken Hyman's general supervision. Once each movie had premiered exclusively on our own network it could then be sold in all the various markets, expanding well beyond traditional theatrical and TV, although we could never have visualised the vast potential in store from DVDs today. The other thing at the heart of the project was sport. Precisely as was later proved by Rupert Murdoch, the two things closest to the average couch-potato's heart are movies and Monday Night Football. Our plan was to concentrate on these two areas as hard as we could, and to get broadcasting rights to every kind of sport imaginable; not just major league football, baseball, basketball and hockey, but English soccer, even cricket, horse-racing, rodeos, car-racing of all kinds. Even certain kinds of gambling like poker could be turned into a spectator sport, we decided, and we began exploratory discussions through our contacts with the MGM Grand. I myself sincerely hoped that something advantageous could be arranged with my favourite race-track at Santa Anita, involving at the very least our own private box! Ted Turner took an interest in our consortium with a view to providing news slots between the other programmes.

It was a condition of the licences granted by the FCC that the successful applicants would enter into contracts to build a satellite with construction to start not more than twelve months later. Before long we were being given VIP treatment by the sales force at the Hughes satellite construction facility at Los Angeles International Airport. The red carpet was rolled out as we were given the tour of the production line. There was the small matter of a deposit of $15 million for the satellite contract. Our group had exhausted its entire modest budget on legal fees but we had always thought that once we had the licence, it would be possible to find funding from corporate partners. Yet this proved much harder than I had imagined.

The sums involved were astronomical – $50 million for each satellite, $20 million for the launch, and unlimited capital for programming and promotion. What we were trying to achieve was little short of launching a complete new television network. As well as Ted Turner we had discussions with executives from several major Hollywood studios. Being the holders of a licence at least gave us a certain status which required interested parties to wine and dine us at the finest restaurants in Beverly Hills. As time went by it became clear that funding was proving difficult not only for us but also for even the mighty CBS. We had inside information from Hughes that not a single order had been placed for a satellite. Lobbyists went to work in Washington to put pressure on the Government to increase the budget for COMSAT so that it could make a greater contribution to the overall cost.

Sadly, this had a negative effect. The fact of bringing the huge costs to the notice of Congress resulted in a change of government policy. It was decided that entertainment was less vital than other domestic issues. Within a year of the licences being issued, COMSAT abandoned the concept of Direct Broadcast Satellite systems on the grounds of excessive cost. It would be another ten years, during which greatly improved technology brought the cost down to more realistic levels, before the whole concept of DBS became the reality that it is today. Our group of visionaries, with Presidential help, had a serious taste of the big time and came close to realising the impossible dream. Even the investor felt he had had a run for his money. Close but no cigar!

Not long after this it was my solemn duty to drive the now unemployed Ian Ross to the gates of a vast Beverly Hills mansion where he, rather than taking up residence, was to begin a four-year stint as a Beverly Hills butler.

8

Meeting Ronnie Wood

People get appointed to jobs in a variety of ways, but my engagement as Ronnie Wood's manager took place under circumstances that were positively unreal. While Flipper's was having its run of success in LA I met a number of potential investors who were interested in taking the Flipper's franchise to other cities. When one of them told me he was a personal friend of the Rolling Stones, it seemed at the time no more than an attempt to impress, and anyway his plans for Mexico City and Acapulco came to nothing for want of a suitable building. However, several months later he asked me if I would be interested in becoming Ronnie's Wood's manager. I was embarrassed to have to admit I wasn't even aware that Ronnie was in the Rolling Stones line-up. On being told that Ronnie was about to start a world tour with the Stones I became very interested. This came just at the point when I was setting up my management business, under the name of Overview Business Management, and an important new client was naturally much to be desired.

In order to meet Ronnie I flew from Los Angeles to Philadelphia where the first concert of the 'Tattoo You' tour was about to take place. Having been settled into my hotel, I was told to wait in the lobby of the hotel or in my room until Ronnie was ready to meet me. I sat there for two days while nothing happened. On the day of the first show of the tour I was summoned to a penthouse suite where Ronnie was putting on his stage clothes. I was introduced to this pencil-thin, long-haired rocker who looked as if he hadn't slept for a week (as indeed he probably hadn't). The interview ran as follows. Ronnie shook my hand and said: 'Hello, mate, so you're gonna be my new manager.'

To me this was nothing short of extraordinary. It seemed absurd that I would be asked to take over someone's business affairs without a proper interview or any questions asked about my background or my other clients. I later realised that no one with any sense would have taken Ronnie on when confronted with full knowledge of the state of his affairs. This perhaps accounted for the swiftness of the proceedings. As Ronnie left for the venue I was briefly introduced to his wife Josephine and to Mick and Keith who were waiting for the lift to take them down to the waiting limos.

I had waited two days for a two-minute interview – my first taste of the 'waiting in the lobby' syndrome that is so much a part of rock 'n' roll.

I had been given a ticket for the show and a VIP pass but didn't see Ronnie again until some weeks later. Semi-VIP pass would be more accurate, as it admitted to a hospitality area but not the exclusive backstage area where the Stones prepared for the show. This was my first experience of the Stones playing live and I was hugely impressed with the show and with Ronnie's guitar work. I got back to Los Angeles and sent Ronnie a Power of Attorney which gave me control over his affairs. This was signed, witnessed and sent back to me by return. I still knew nothing of the parlous state of his finances and the chaotic mess surrounding all his business affairs.

The Wood family was living in Los Angeles on Mandeville Canyon. The house had once been lived in by Esther Williams, the swimming star, who drowned there when it was swamped by an enormous mudslide. Like most houses in the area, the Woods' house was equipped with a security alarm system operated by a keypad next to the front door. When I arrived at the house for the first time the keypad was falling to pieces with the cover plate torn off and the works exposed. The door was answered by Jaye Carter, the housekeeper. I asked her what had happened. She told me that Mr and Mrs Wood had made one of their rare sorties into the outside world a few months previously, and returning home late at night couldn't remember the alarm code. So Ronnie had taken a brick to the keypad and destroyed it.

Jaye, a black lady of ample girth, was a combination of cook, nanny, housekeeper and trusted friend to the Wood household. I asked her to give me the mail and any papers with which I might familiarise myself with the Woods' affairs. Jaye said, 'You'd better take a look at this', and led me to a large cupboard which, when opened, disgorged an avalanche of unopened letters onto the floor. There were hundreds, of which a good few were from an attorney in Los Angeles who was representing Ronnie. Such was Ronnie's aversion to business matters that he would not even open a letter. After a few days of investigation and a meeting with the attorney, I found a very sorry state of affairs.

Far from being the millionaire rock star I had imagined, Ronnie was on the verge of financial collapse. The house was threatened with foreclosure for failure to make mortgage pay-ments, no tax returns had been filed for several years for Ronnie or his corporation and there was a mountain of unpaid bills. It is true he was about to embark on a Stones tour, but he was on a weekly wage and didn't share in tour profits. Furthermore, in order to raise much-needed cash he had sold his entitlement to his share of royalties from the Stones album *Emotional Rescue*. A large publishing advance had also been taken and largely dissipated in the financing of a New Barbarians tour which Ronnie put together to promote his solo album.

The Barbarians had toured with the luxury of a private jet, something which Ronnie could ill afford. Other more unsavoury matters came to light. His previous manager was facing very serious criminal charges relating to the manufacture of pipe bombs. A number of drug dealers were queuing up for payment. To my dismay I realised that I had landed myself in a very worrying and complicated situation.

One of my first jobs was to negotiate a settlement with the attorney who held all the contracts and files relating to Ronnie's affairs. He submitted a huge bill, of which a large part consisted of charges for the hundreds of letters he had written to Ronnie which had been left unopened in the Mandeville Canyon house. Many of them were form letters, simply enclosing a bill or a royalty statement, but for each one he had charged a large fee. As the letters were coming thick and fast his bill was running up like a taxi meter. I had noticed the white Rolls-Royce with personalised number plate outside the lawyer's office and could see where the money was going. I persuaded him to take a discount and payment by instalments. After reviewing dozens of files I set about clearing up the mess. I appointed accountants to write up the books of Ronnie's company and prepare long-overdue tax returns. As Ronnie was on tour I only saw him for a few days now and then when I joined the tour. Because of the track record of managers who had come and gone before me, it was a long time before I gained acceptance by any of the entourage.

As the tour progressed and Ronnie's pay cheque came in regularly I was able to deal with the most pressing problems. After a year or so I moved to New York where I opened an office on the corner of 62nd street and Lexington Avenue. I was juggling several jobs at once. The winding down of Flipper's and the disposal of the site took me back to Los Angeles on a regular basis. Denny Cordell had moved to Ireland to train racehorses, leaving me as acting president of his record label. And I had the management company in New York. Although I was busy, I did find the time to go to six shows on the North American leg of the tour.

One incident gave me a scare when the Stones performed at Giants Stadium in New York. The stage for the 'Tattoo You' tour was on two levels. Charlie Watts and his drumkit were positioned on the upper level about ten feet higher than the front of the stage where Mick and Keith moved around while Bill Wyman remained rooted to his spot. Ronnie would occasionally run to the upper level for a short burst. In a completely unrehearsed move that took Mick by surprise, Ronnie, guitar in hand and fuelled by vodka, leapt from the top level onto Mick's shoulders. It was a miracle that Mick remained upright and that no one was hurt.

After a break for Christmas the tour moved on to Japan. It was in Tokyo that I first had dinner with Prince Rupert Loewenstein, the overall business manager and financial adviser to the Stones. Prince Rupert was a former merchant banker of the highest calibre. I wanted to get on with him because I knew I would have to negotiate a new deal with Prince Rupert to make Ronnie a profit-sharing member of the group. Fortunately we did get on well, thanks to a mutual interest in gastronomy and fine wines and shared recollections of memorable meals we had enjoyed at some of the best restaurants in Europe. There was another tenuous though somewhat mystifying link. Many years earlier I had been invited by a schoolfriend to stay the weekend at his house in the Cotswolds, called Biddestone Manor, where I had an unforgettable experience. After a heavy Saturday night dinner with enough alcohol to send me into a deep sleep I retired to bed and immediately passed out. One hour later I was awakened with an inexplicable feeling of unease. In normal circumstances it would have taken an atomic explosion to rouse me from my inebriated slumber. I was certain there was an unpleasant, almost evil, presence in my room. I was so frightened that I kept the light on for the rest of the night.

By an extraordinary coincidence, I now discovered, Prince Rupert was now living at Biddestone Manor. I recounted my experience from twenty years earlier. Prince Rupert asked, 'Were you in the second bedroom on the right at the top of the stairs?' I confirmed I was. 'No one can sleep easily in that room,' he continued. That, it would appear, has been my one and only paranormal experience.

Broadly speaking, there are two separate functions which performing artists, sportsmen and the like choose to have handled by managers. These are personal management and business management.

The personal manager is closely involved with the creative side of the artist's activities. Perhaps the best example of this type of manager was Brian Epstein, who managed the Beatles from the time he discovered them in the Cavern Club in Liverpool until his untimely death in 1967. Others may have recognised their talent but he was alone in spotting the potential market for their records. It was his money that paid for a demo album, which was rejected by almost every British record company until the tiny Parlophone label offered a deal. In time, Brian created a new image of the Beatles as clean-cut young men, managing to get them to wear suits and even stopping them from swearing and smoking on stage. Every aspect of their publicity was carefully monitored by him. In the early years he paid all their expenses, recouping his losses later on from the millions that poured in. In addition he became a close personal friend of the band members. On the financial side he employed accountants and lawyers to set up companies in order to reduce their tax bills. Once Beatles earnings reached a certain figure, Brian took a management fee of 25 percent, giving him more than any individual band member and considerably more than the usual 10 percent that managers took at the time.

Business managers, on the other hand, have a less intimate relationship with their clients and are less concerned with the artistic and creative side of their lives. They will often be accountants, whose task it is to take care of all financial aspects of the client's life from tax, insurance, investments, contracts and disputes to the day-to-day payment of living expenses, household bills and travel arrangements. They relieve their clients of the burden of paperwork, phone calls and other distractions, allowing them to worry only about their more important artistic endeavours. Business managers don't perform all these functions themselves. They use lawyers, travel agents, bankers, stockbrokers and so no to provide their clients with a one-stop service. Their fees are in the range of 7 to 10 percent of gross earnings.

Allen Klein is credited with creating the concept of business management within the music industry. Adept at figures, his speciality was going through the books of the large record companies on an artist's behalf and digging up royalties which were due but unpaid. Royalty accounting is a tangled thicket that contains provisions for reserves, numerous foreign deals and questionable expenses, and the major labels were past masters at sitting on royalties which should have been paid to artists. Allen Klein and his company ABKCO managed the remarkable feat of persuading both Mick Jagger on behalf of the Stones and John Lennon for the Beatles that he should take over their business management (though not at the same time). He lasted about five years with each group, and in each case the relationship ended with extensive litigation from which he emerged the winner. To this day ABKCO owns the rights to some of the earliest and most important Rolling Stones recordings.

The partnership of Elton John and his long-time personal manager John Reid was another that ended in court. Elton sued Reid and his accountants for allowing him to spend tens of millions in a couple of years, but lost the case and had to pay several millions more in legal fees.

Don Arden was a manager of the old school. Completely ruthless, and not afraid to settle any dispute with violence, he had a talent for discovering new bands and frequently helped them on the way to stardom. Along the road all their earnings would somehow disappear into Arden's companies. The tables were turned on him eventually when his daughter Sharon married Ozzie Osbourne and took over his management from Don. After that the two sides had nothing to do with each other for many years.

The most famous manager of all was 'Colonel' Tom Parker, who was Elvis Presley's personal and business manager throughout Elvis's professional life. The Colonel had total control over all Elvis's business dealings and directed his musical career in the way that best suited himself. Not only did he take 50 percent of all Elvis's earnings, he also controlled merchandising and other spin-offs to the extent that by the end of Elvis's life the manager was earning more than the artist.

Elvis never toured in Europe although he could have sold out any stadium in any country. The Colonel preferred to keep Elvis working in a series of second-rate movies even though a world tour would have made him and the Colonel a lot more money. When I met Elvis's legendary lead guitarist Scotty Moore at Ronnie Wood's studio in the '80s, he told me the reason why Elvis never toured abroad. The Colonel, who was of Dutch origin, did not have a US passport and lived in fear of deportation if he applied for one.

In recent times, artists have proved much more interested in controlling their own careers. By and large the days of the manager controlling the artist are over. But in certain areas the manager can still have a pivotal role, booking tours, negotiating deals and taking care of business. And there is a certain kind of 'concept' group (the Spice Girls being the most obvious example) which owes its very existence to management.

The best managers are those the general public never hear about. They just keep providing a satisfactory service for their clients over the years. Those who make the headlines are usually in the news either because they have run off with their client's money or because they are locked in a court battle over the contract. With all my clients I never had a written contact. We agreed a fee based on earnings –usually 10 percent – and shook hands on it. I took the view that if the client wasn't happy with the service he should be free to walk away. I don't believe in going to court to resolve disputes.

In the case of Ronnie Wood there was an overlap between the roles of business manager and personal manager. In addition to taking care of business I helped Ronnie establish a second career as a successful artist. I encouraged him to create images we could issue as limited editions as well as selling originals. He was reluctant to part with many originals, pre-ferring to keep them in his own collection, but the limited edition print business grew sufficiently large to keep him going in the years when the Stones were not touring and there was little revenue from music. I was closely involved in the setting up of many exhibitions, the creation of relationships with galleries around the world and the production of two books of Ronnie's art. My personal duties also included periods of baby-sitting, when it was my task to stay with Ronnie while he was drying out, to ensure he stayed on the wagon.

9

Life with the Woods

Rock stars and models find each other irresistible, and Ronnie Wood and Josephine were no exception. When they met in 1977 it was, according to Ronnie, love at first sight. At the time Jo, as she has always been known, was married with a young son and Ronnie was married to his first wife Krissie, also with a son. To complicate matters, Ronnie was having a passionate affair with Pattie Boyd and Krissie was involved with Jimmy Page. Ronnie and Jo ran off together to Paris and have been together ever since.

It's hardly news that rock stars are not short of opportunities to meet women, whether it be on tour or in the recording studio. Any number of rockers have cited this as their main motive for wanting to be a star in the first place – to get girls. Going on tour was an opportunity to leave wives and girl-friends at home and to enjoy the pleasures available to a rock band travelling the world. But Jo was cleverer than most other girls and she never let Ronnie out of her sight. She was the only Stones girl who always went on every tour, so much so that she was put on the payroll as Ronnie's PA and wardrobe assistant. When the Stones went abroad to record a studio album, Jo would set up house in Paris or wherever the recording was taking place. Although relatively new to the drug scene when she met Ronnie, by the time I met them in 1981 she had joined Ronnie in his dual addiction of cocaine and alcohol. To her credit, she had the strength of character to beat the addiction in later years and was an enormous help to Ronnie when he needed to clean up his act so as to function as a regular member of the Stones.

When I first opened an office in New York's East Side in 1982, Ronnie and Jo were living on the West Side. In a moment of temporary insanity Ronnie moved into a mid-town hotel with the actress Kelly LeBrock, star of *The Woman in Red*. I acted as go-between relaying messages between Jo and Ronnie. Jo was very cool about the situation and went on with life as normal until, after a week or so, Ronnie came home. After that ten years were to go by before she allowed Ronnie to take a trip with me to Ireland on our own. This was an important precedent which, once set, was often repeated and we were allowed off the leash for frequent solo trips.

Much fun was had on these occasions and Ronnie kept in touch by phone with several Dublin girls until Jo caught him one time on the phone to one of them and put an end to it. I kept the numbers of the girls we met in my phone under code names – Prado for the one who had been a student in Madrid, Gaz for the one with big gazongas, Teach for obvious reasons. Jo was smart enough not to make a big deal out of it. But she may have realised then that I was not to be trusted with Ronnie in Ireland, and I believe it was around this time that she decided I should be retired and replaced as manager by her son Jamie.

By the time the 'Tattoo You' tour reached France in the summer of 1982 I felt I had become accepted by the entourage as a whole. Keith's personal manager, Jane Rose, made a foray with me to the casino in Monte Carlo, where I was able to demonstrate the finer points of blackjack. At the end of the tour the Woods moved to New York, first renting in the Village and later buying a house on the West Side that my girlfriend Julie found for them. Ronnie had a studio in his basement and lived a nocturnal existence. The house was kept going by their loyal housekeeper Jaye, who had moved with them from Los Angeles.

With mortgage payments, wages, and limousine bills to pay plus an expensive addiction to feed, the monthly outgoings were high. The tour had rescued Ronnie from financial collapse but we had to find another source of income to keep afloat between tours. As it turned out there was not to be another tour for seven years. It was during this period that Ronnie's art career was launched. He was an accomplished artist and had been to art college but had not previously taken his art to a commercial level. I took him to a studio in San Francisco where he perfected the art of making woodcuts. There followed an exhibition of his work in the US, the first of many.

Real success came when I arranged an art tour in Japan with exhibitions in several cities. The buyers were mostly young Stones fans. In every city we had a reception where buyers of prints could be photographed shaking Ronnie's hand or getting a kiss. At one point we visited the South Island where we stayed in an ancient Japanese inn complete with natural hot springs. In our rooms were laid out traditional Japanese costumes which we donned for a twelve-course feast that was served in our rooms Later, when we decided to go down to the bar for a drink dressed in our imperial robes, we discovered to our embarrassment that the other guests, all Japanese, were wearing blue jeans and T-shirts. We looked complete idiots.

At Fukuoka the tour organiser and gallery owner insisted on a karaoke evening at a very exclusive club. This was something our hosts took very seriously, and my version of 'Danny Boy' was an embarrassment to all present.

As well as the art exhibitions, there were a number of one-off appearances which brought in much-needed dollars. One less than successful event was 'An Evening with Ronnie Wood' at New York Town Hall presented by the Learning Annexe, who paid well for such events. The evening was not to be a musical one. Ronnie was to talk about his career and answer questions from the audience. I knew we had a problem when he strode onto the stage carrying a bottle of Jack Daniels of which a fair amount had already disappeared. Matters were not helped by a small but vociferous group of hecklers who constantly interrupted with shouts of 'Seven Days' or 'Ooh-La-La' in an attempt to get Ronnie to perform one of his hits. The evening descended into farce when the stage lights failed halfway through the show. The bottle of Jack Daniels was polished off and we beat a hasty retreat from the Town Hall.

Ronnie had a few interests outside the world of music and art, of which one was tennis. We went to the Volvo Masters indoor tennis as guests of John McEnroe, who was a good friend of Ronnie's. In return for front row seats at the tennis, Ronnie used to give McEnroe guitar lessons. McEnroe took his rock band very seriously, an attitude which, sadly for him, was not shared by anyone else in the music business.

The Rolling Stones connection opened many doors. Studio 54, though not quite the force it had been before its founder Steve Rubell went to gaol, was still the number one disco in New York. The owners threw a party for Josephine Wood's birthday so as to get some celebrities through the door. From then on I was given the key to the VIP entrance to the place. Groups of young would-be models were part of the scenery at Studio 54 and I took my place on the list of men-about-town who were invited as escorts. This, as may be imagined, was an arduous burden but I bore it manfully without complaining.

With the help of Ronnie's name it was easy enough to get a table reservation in any restaurant, but his nocturnal schedule didn't allow for many dinners. He would get up in the afternoon and after a proper English breakfast would settle down for some TV before starting the night's session in the studio.

Often I had to get by with very little sleep, as I had to be ready for work in the office every morning after a night in the studio. I tried to get Ronnie interested in the theatre. I took him and Josephine to see George C. Scott in the Noel Coward play *Hay Fever*. Fifteen minutes after the curtain went up Ronnie was asleep. He woke up for a quick drink during the interval and then settled down to sleep again. That was the last of our cultural outings in New York.

One summer we took a joint rental of a holiday house in the Hamptons at Sag Harbour. The house was elegantly decorated with some fine furniture. Keith Richards came to stay for a few days while he was working on his solo album. After a few days Keith and Ronnie had covered every flat surface in the living room with empty glasses, overflowing ashtrays, half-opened bottles and the assorted debris of a 48-hour session without sleep. Noticing the cigarette burns on the tables, wine stains on the carpet and a couple of broken chairs, I summoned up the courage to say something about the damage. 'Stop worrying, Nick, it's only a rental,' said Keith as he stubbed out another cigarette butt on the carpet. That became something of a catch-phrase with Ronnie over the years.

During the next couple of years Ronnie's art output was more prolific and he spent some time working with Peter Max, a very successful pop artist, in his studio. Art sales kept the wolf from the door. One of his best portraits was of John Belushi, whom I met a few times at his apartment in New York. Belushi was a physical wreck. He looked years older than his actual age of twenty-eight. Hugely overweight and sweating profusely, he would ingest long lines of cocaine washed down with large vodkas. He said little and stared constantly at Josephine Wood, with whom he professed to be deeply in love. There was no evidence that the feeling was reciprocated.

In 1985 the Stones started work on a new studio album at

Olympia Studios in Paris. I was greatly relieved since they always followed the release of a new album with a tour. Prince Rupert had accepted the principle that Ronnie would have a share of the profit from touring, so I thought the future was secure. Hence it came as a huge blow when, before the 'Dirty Work' album was finished, Mick announced that there would be no Stones tour because he wanted to concentrate on his solo career.

The Woods moved back to London. Phil Carson, an experienced manager in the live music business, was taken on to help generate some work for Ronnie. Phil was able to put together a world tour with the legendary Bo Diddley, financed by the Japanese giant Panasonic. The 'Gunslingers' tour, as it was called, was a great success and resulted in the release of a videotape of a live show from the Ritz in New York. As well as being one of the cornerstones of original rock 'n' roll, Bo was a great character and very proud of the fact that in real life he was a deputy sheriff in his home town. He invariably came on stage wearing his sheriff's hat.

Phil Carson was not around for long. For reasons known only to herself, Mrs Wood took against him and he parted company with Ronnie after the tour. So there was still a need to find further sources of income for Ronnie. I had been approached earlier in 1987 by the British American Chamber of Commerce in Miami for Ronnie to get involved with a live music venue in South Beach. The result was the nightclub Woody's on the Beach. David Giles, an Englishman living in Miami, had acquired a couple of derelict hotels, the Savoy and the Arlington, on the beach side of Ocean Avenue not far from the famous restaurant Joe's Stone Crabs. Although the bedrooms were uninhabitable, there was enough of a usable reception area in the Savoy to create a bar, an art gallery and a sound stage which could be viewed by an audience of several hundred.

Ronnie and family and his brother Art flew in for a two-week party for the opening. Ronnie had assembled a house band including Bobby Keys from the Stones brass section and Ian McClagan from The Faces. Rather unwisely, David Giles had given over his house in Miami to the Wood party. The wine cellar was drunk dry and the neighbours were kept up all night with the constant party-going.

Woody's had a press opening with two shows on 19 and 20 December 1987, when Ronnie played along with Bo Diddley. Then it closed until the official opening on New Year's Eve, using the house band. This was in front of a select audience that included Gloria and Emilio Estefan, Bjorn Borg, Vitas Gerulaitis and John McEnroe.

Other notable performers who appeared at Woody's were Ray Charles, Willie Dixon, Jerry Lee Lewis (who played on the day he was made personally bankrupt by the IRS), the Neville Brothers, Buddy Guy, Toots and the Maytalls, Ziggy Marley, Spencer Davis, and Katy Segal of *Married with Children* fame. All the live performances by named artists were sell-outs, including several nights with Paul Shaeffer. Ronnie was only required to appear twice a year and he had the benefit of a permanent gallery of his artwork.

The opening of the art gallery took place during the daytime and involved a ceremony at which Ronnie was given the keys to the City of South Beach by the Mayor, after which Don Johnson of 'Miami Vice' performed the ribbon-cutting. He brought Ronnie a handgun as a somewhat unsuitable present.

The popularity of the venue brought problems. Miami licensing laws allowed clubs to remain open for business until 5 a.m. At closing time large numbers of noisy revellers spilled out into the surrounding streets. The club was in the Art Deco district and didn't have its own parking lot. So there was much noisy slamming of car doors as the valets delivered cars from surrounding streets. Local residents repeatedly filed complaints at City Hall. South Beach in the '80s was not at all the place it is today. It was largely residential and many of the locals were pensioners. In fact Woody's was a few years before its time. The curtain finally fell when a delegation of local residents stormed the mayor's office and demanded that its licence be withdrawn. The official order specified that Woody's be closed for 'noise pollution'. For a brief time the club relocated to New York but again there were noise problems and it was forced to close.

Thanks to Ronnie acting as intermediary, Mick and Keith began talking to each other again in 1988. This resulted in a new studio album and the 'Steel Wheels' tour, which kicked off in 1989. I had negotiated a contract for Ronnie with Prince Rupert which gave him a decent share of the tour profits. By the time the tour started the Woods had moved to London and the problems that I inherited in 1981 had been cleared up.

10

Stones Tour Diary

The tour diary which follows is typical of a few weeks on tour although it is made up of a composite of events, people and incidents from several Rolling Stones tours.

No matter where he is in the world Keith Richards has two essential requirements. First he has to have a snooker table set up in the backstage area, so he can enjoy a few frames before each show. The second concerns dinner. He has his food set out in his tuning room, an inner sanctum where only fellow band members and special guests are invited. That food must include a freshly cooked shepherd's pie for Keith's personal consumption. Alabama, Georgia is no different, except that in Keith's eyes a crime of epic proportions has been committed. Someone has broken the crust on the pie and helped themselves to a sizeable portion before Keith has entered the room.

I become aware that something is wrong when Keith's PA puts out an urgent message on the walkie-talkies carried backstage. Keith is demanding to see the Tour Manager, the Catering Manager and the Head of Security in his tuning room immediately. By the time they arrive Keith is in an apoplectic vodka-fuelled rage and insisting on an immediate enquiry. It is inconceivable to him that someone should have had the gall to start eating his pie before him.

There is little time before the show starts and Keith needs to be calmed down before he goes on stage. My hope that the whole matter will be forgotten during the performance is not fulfilled. Keith leaves the stage still incandescent with rage and orders an enquiry to be set up immediately the members of the entourage arrive back at the hotel. Anyone, apart from fellow band members, who has been backstage is to be interrogated in Keith's suite. Fortunately for me I have a solid alibi but by now Keith's fury is such that no one in their right mind would own up for fear of being assaulted by him. The next morning, with still no sign of a confession from the guilty party, Keith fires both the Head of Security and the Tour Manager. However, since the tour cannot go on without their services they are swiftly reinstated by the promoter.

It is October in Florida. Two months and twenty-five shows have gone by since the first show in August. There is a week's break, for the duration of which Keith Richards and Ronnie Wood are staying in a rented house in Palm Beach. Staying in the house alongside family members and personal assistants is one Freddie Sessler, who describes himself as the world's oldest groupie but is also renowned for his ability to supply any sort of pill without prescription. I am staying at the nearby Breakers Hotel, spending evenings and most of the nights at the rented house and trying to catch up on my sleep during the day. The first few days have passed relatively quietly but on Wednesday Keith and Ronnie get involved in a marathon song-writing session which is to last more than 48 hours. A mixture of vodka and cocaine plus pills, known as Sessler's helpers, keep both of them wired up.

Iron man Keith sees sleep as a weakness and heaps insults on anybody who needs to go to bed before he is ready. I am able to slip away in the early mornings without attracting too much attention but by Friday with a show scheduled for the following day we finally manage to persuade both of them to take to their beds. There is one problem. Keith is so overhyped from his intake of the past few days that he's unable to sleep. Sessler is summoned and administers a powerful sleeping pill which has the desired effect. The private jet which is due to transport everyone to Orlando is scheduled to leave at 2.00 p.m. the following day, giving Ronnie and Keith plenty of time to recover. I am feeling more relaxed as I go back to the Breakers to have a night's sleep for a change. But when I return to the house the following morning I realise immediately that something has gone seriously wrong.

Ronnie is fine, wide awake and having his usual fry-up, but Larry, Keith's PA, has been unable to wake Keith. No amount of shaking and shouting can get him to stir. It later transpires that there were enough barbiturates in the sleeping pill to anaesthetise a horse. The telephone rings. It is the tour manager calling from Orlando to make sure that Ronnie and Keith are on schedule. I brush aside his concerns and hang up as soon as possible. While I have been talking on the telephone Keith has finally been woken up by the simple method of having iced water poured all over him, but there is a further problem. So deep was the drug-induced sleep that Keith has remained motionless for hours with his full weight on his right arm. Circulation to the arm has been cut off and he cannot move it. At this point Keith declares he is going back to sleep and does just that. Now there is a serious time problem. We are going to be at least two hours late taking off but we cannot leave without Keith. Can we strap him on to his mattress and transport him like that, or can Sessler undo the damage? It is Sessler who finally manages to wake Keith and this time persuades him to take another pill to get the adrenaline running. In the meantime one of the assistants has been massaging Keith's arm trying to get the circulation going. Meanwhile in Orlando, where the temperature is close to 90°, the stadium is filling up with 50,000 fans. Mick and Charlie have had to hold the sound check without Ronnie and Keith.

The tour manager has stopped ringing but the promoter Bill Graham has been bawling at anyone stupid enough to pick up the telephone. Finally, after several hours of work on Keith's arm, the circulation has been restored and we can leave for the airport, but not before Keith has had his usual afternoon breakfast of red wine. Limos are waiting on the tarmac at Orlando to rush Keith and Ronnie to the stadium.

By now the start of the show is two hours late and the audience is restless. As Keith's limo pulls into the backstage area and Keith starts to get out, the promoter Bill Graham charges up to Keith cursing him to hell for leaving the audience sweating so long. Bill is boiling over with rage and his tirade is endless. Keith suddenly snaps and turning back to the limo he shouts at Bill: 'I don't have to listen to this shit. You play – I'm going back to Palm Beach.' So saying, he thrusts his Fender into Bill's arms and gets back into the limo. Bill's outburst is choked off in an instant. His entire demeanour changes and he is now imploring Keith to get out of the limo. After letting Bill sweat for a couple of minutes Keith complies and joins the rest of the band backstage. Although very late the concert is hugely successful. The band take their bow after the usual two-song encore and are already in blacked-out vans leaving the stadium while the audience is on its feet applauding and calling for more.

Back at the hotel the band members retire to their respective suites. Charlie Watts, who is teetotal and vegetarian, settles in for a quiet night after his usual massage. Mick Jagger has a rendezvous known only to his security man.

Keith will spend the night listening to music with only a few close friends for company. His suite is not accessible unless an invitation has been issued. When issued, it has the force of a royal command. Ronnie's suite, on the other hand, is known as party central. All night, every night the door is open to anyone who wants a drink and more. Of course, security is present to keep out undesirables but in every city Ronnie's party friends seem to come out of the woodwork.

The suite overflows with alcohol and is thick with the smoke of cigarettes and other substances. Coke is available and on this occasion one of Ronnie's 'friends' wanders into the bedroom and spies a pile of white powder on the bedside table. Rolling a 20-dollar bill he helps himself to a generous line and rejoins the party. Later on he compliments his host on the quality of his blow. When I see Ronnie a few minutes later he is laughing so much he can barely speak. The friend has been informed that Ronnie administered a pedicure to himself earlier in the evening and he has succeeded in snorting the dead skin from the soles of Ronnie's feet.

At 5 a.m. the party is still in full swing. I try to keep my own alcohol intake to reasonable levels but the assorted guests and freeloaders have no such inhibitions. There will be no sleep for those in party central that night. Ronnie and I will catch a few hours in the morning before an afternoon press conference and a further show that evening.

Although the afternoon is hot a heavy cloud cover is building up and storms are forecast. The show will go on whatever the weather. The stage is uncovered but the equipment will operate in even the heaviest downpour. Keith has designated himself as the resident weather man and he arrives at the stadium carrying an ornately carved wooden staff from Jamaica which he claims is endowed with magical qualities. He steps outside and waves his staff at the rain clouds, all the while muttering voodoo incarnations and cursing the god of rain. An hour later the clouds have cleared away and the show goes ahead under clear skies.

After the show the band and entourage go straight from

the stadium to the tour jet for the short flight to Atlanta. Mick, Keith, Charlie and Ronnie sit up front on the tour jet. Members of the entourage are seated further back down the plane in accordance with their status, promoter and manager nearest to the front and security at the back. On arrival at the hotel the band is taken through the service entrance to avoid the throng of fans waiting outside. After settling in the band members resume their usual pattern. Mick has a rendezvous, Charlie goes to bed, Keith cranks up the music and Ronnie opens party central in his suite.

The next day is a free day for the band. None of them will be seen until the evening but I have meetings with promoters, record label representatives and art dealers interested in exhibiting Ronnie's work. This will go on for most of the day and I am hoping I will be overlooked when the invitations are issued for party central that evening, so I can get a rare early night. A telephone call dashes my hopes and it is 6 a.m. before I shake myself loose from Ronnie's collection of friends old and new.

At the stadium the following day there is a larger than usual number of VIPs with backstage passes. Many are sportsmen from the Atlanta baseball and football teams. The backstage area, the décor of which is the responsibility of the local promoter, has been decorated with a Halloween theme and the catering is more lavish than usual. There is a choice of oriental cuisine as well as the usual international fare. The selection of wines on offer is also well above average. The entourage and the guests are enjoying this lavish hospitality before the show. Some of the band members and musicians mingle with the guests. One person who shows no interest whatsoever in what is on offer is Keith Richards.

Bobby Keys is the best sax player in the business who has played all the Stones tours and has been a sideman for just about every rock 'n' roll great from the Everly Brothers and Buddy Holly to Eric Clapton and George Harrison. With six ex-wives and a son called Huckleberry, Bobby is the most entertaining guy on the tour. His weakness for a pretty face has caused him trouble all his life. We are in Tokyo and have a night off so we decide to go to the Rippongi district for some fun. The early part of the evening is spent at the Red Dragon Bar, where the preferred drink is a fiery brew poured from a bottle containing a pickled lizard with dragon-like features. Duly warmed up, we move to a hostess bar where scantily clad hostesses are performing on trapezes over our heads. After a few hours I decide to go back to the Ocura Hotel but cannot persuade Bobby to leave with me. He is hypnotised by the performers.

By closing time, so I learn the following day, Bobby has had several more cocktails but has now forgotten the name of the hotel where the Stones are staying. His southern drawl does not help his discussions with a number of taxi drivers, of whom none speaks a word of English and all look blankly at him when he directs them to take him to the Stones' hotel. He only gets back hours later after being driven around Tokyo for half the night to all the large hotels until he recognises the Ocura. The taxi fare has burned up a week's salary.

Bobby is on a substantial salary for the duration of the tour but like everyone else he is responsible for extras such his room service bill. By the end of the tour he has run up so many extras that he is in debt. On the next tour I try to help him with his finances. This proves to be an impossible task. He manages to break the record for largest room service bill ever run up in one night. He meets a lovely girl and is desperate to impress her. She has a liking for champagne so he decides to try a champagne bath. He orders up the hotel's entire stock of Dom Perignon and fills the bathtub. When I ask him how it went down with the girl he replies laconically: 'She was impressed all right.'

There is nowhere quite like Japan. Fans will wait all day and night outside the hotel for a glimpse of a band member and will give anything for an autograph. I am in the lobby of Ocura hotel where the head of security has introduced me to a Japanese businessman who wants me to deliver a letter to Prince Rupert. His English is not great but I understand that he is trying to sell water which comes from Tibet, collected from a source once blessed by the Dalai Lama. This seems an unlikely venture but he is so polite that I have tea with him in the hotel lobby. We agree to meet the following day. When we meet again he brings with him a bottle of the special water and a written proposal. He tells me that he has a gift for my mother or girlfriend and hands me an elaborately wrapped package which he says contains a gold necklace. He also says he has a gift for me and nods his head in the direction of the bank of elevators.

I have no idea what he means. All I can see is three Japanese girls sitting there. But he takes me over to these three beauties and tells me to choose one and take her up to my room. It is considered extremely insulting to refuse a gift in Japan so I get into the lift with an exquisite Japanese model who speaks not a word of English and who giggles like a schoolgirl. No sooner am I in my room than the telephone rings. It is Ronnie calling from Keith's suite. My presence is requested as I am leaving Tokyo the following day. A request from Keith is a royal command, so I have to say goodbye without the chance of unwrapping my present and make my way to Keith's room. There I will have to stay until morning because Keith never goes to bed before sunrise and it is not done to leave until Keith is ready to retire.

The night is spent discussing a wide variety of subjects. Keith is surprisingly articulate, given his mainly liquid diet. He is also well-read, with a library covering a broad range from Tolstoy to Winston Churchill. He spends hours comparing the finer points of English TV comedy and can quote verbatim the entire series of 'Hancock's Half Hour' and every word of all the Tommy Cooper shows. Finally the sun is up and I have to leave for the airport.

Eventually, after 114 shows, the tour is coming to an end. The girls in the entourage have planned a surprise for the last show. There are about a dozen of them who have been on the road throughout the tour, taking care of wardrobe, make-up, catering, tour accounts, PR and so on. The front row of seats at every show is left empty in order to create a barrier between the crowd and the stage. The girls are given permission to watch the show from these seats. During the final number, at a given signal, they all open their tops and display their breasts. The band on stage see twenty-four tits wiggling at them. Reaction is mixed. The band is amused, but not so Prince Rupert. There is even talk of tour bonuses being reduced, but in the end everyone manages to laugh it off.

11

Stones Corporate

I have been asked many times what it's like to be on tour with the Stones. It's not a question that can be simply answered in a few words because there are so many aspects to a world tour. It is probably fair to say, however, that reality is rather different from what most people imagine.

Journalists write with admiration about the rigours of touring the world to perform a two-hour show more than a hundred times in a dozen different countries over a year or so, particularly for a bunch of dinosaurs. Yet a Stones tour schedule is far less demanding than that of the stars of a typical West End or Broadway musical that plays eight shows a week, every week. The Stones perform only three or four times a week. Every few weeks there is a week's break with no shows at all. Even taking into account sound checks, meet-and-greets, and the occasional compulsory function, the working week is hardly onerous.

The organisation and logistics of a Stones world tour are such that no detail is overlooked in attending to the comfort and well-being of the band. The band members are pampered as if they were royalty. They don't have to give a second's thought to travel arrangements, comfort, food, drink, accommodation and security. The personal needs of each individual are taken care of by an army of helpers who form part of what is known as 'the entourage'. Although I often travelled with this entourage, I was never present for the entirety of a tour. I would pick and choose the countries or places I wanted to visit and join the tour for a week or so at a time. My job usually involved arranging an exhibition of Ronnie Wood's art to coincide with the Stones shows in, say, Tokyo or Buenos Aires. These exhibitions did not have the wholehearted support of the rest of the band, but as Ronnie was not an original member of the Rolling Stones he received a smaller share of the tour profits than the others. I saw nothing wrong in trying to boost his income from art sales.

Another reason why I could only manage to be with the tour a week or so at a time was the fact that in the Woods' suite every night was party night, and whilst it was fun once in a while to spend the night with a bunch of lunatic Brazilians in San Paulo listening to blaring music and imbibing to excess, it was not something I could do night after night. The musicians and crazy guests could sleep it off the next day but I usually had business to attend to, which meant getting up in the morning. If I was present during any particular week of the tour it was expected that I would put in an appearance at party central.

The entourage includes personal assistants, PR agents, make-up artists, wardrobe keepers, personal trainers, sidemen musicians, back-up vocalists, travel and ticket agents, promoter and management, accountants, sound and lighting engineers plus family members of the band who join the tour from time to time. At any given time there might be up to a hundred people making up the entourage and their guests. All these people are accommodated in five-star hotels wherever the Stones are playing. In addition each band member has his own security guard, a massive presence whose job it is to sit outside the band member's suite and keep out uninvited guests. Security will also accompany any band member who leaves the hotel to go to a restaurant or visit a place of interest. For Mick it might be a social event, for Charlie Watts a cultural inspection of the local architecture, for Ronnie Wood an art gallery, and for Keith Richards probably nothing at all as he tended to stay in his suite listening to music.

There is one member of the entourage who is rarely seen by the others. That is the person whose sole job it is to be one step ahead in the next city where the Stones are to perform to ensure that all is in readiness for the band's arrival. Each band member had his own particular requirements for the fitting out of his hotel suite. Keith Richards has an aversion to hotel lighting, so his suite must be equipped with lamps, each of which is shrouded with a colourful scarf. For many years Ronnie had to have a huge fridge installed and filled with cans of draught Guinness. Mrs Wood had her own cooking facilities in the suite so she could prepare organic food rather than order from room service. Mick and Charlie, who enjoy their sleep, will have suites as far away as possible from Keith and Ronnie, who are night people.

Such is the volume of the music that can be heard through the night from these two that their suites must be isolated from the other rooms. The rooms on the floor below are un-lettable except to the totally deaf.

The bars must be stocked with the right bottles, and the hotel kitchen must be ready to produce special food around the clock. Even in the furthest corners of the world British essentials such as baked beans, HP sauce and PG Tips tea must be on hand. The suites will be equipped with high end music and video systems, often used to replay a night's performance.

The planning and preparation for each tour starts a year or more in advance. The promoter must first come up with financial guarantees based on the booking of stadiums and other venues around the world. In order to accommodate the largest possible number of spectators most shows take place in outdoor venues. The weather dictates the routing of the tour. North America in the autumn, Europe in the summer, Australia in their summer and so on. Sponsors must be found and signed up for different territories. There is always an album to be released to coincide with the tour, so the record label will be intimately involved with tour planning. Managers, lawyers, tax planners and accountants are kept busy for months.

The band members decide a theme for the tour and the set and lighting designers get to work. Rehearsals go on for weeks while the stage is being constructed. Every number which might be played on the tour is rehearsed and choreographed. In addition to the entourage there is an army of riggers, technicians, lighting and camera operators – perhaps another two hundred people who will join the tour. For months prior to the start the band members will give interviews to press and TV to promote the tour.

The moment of greatest tension is right before the first show. Will the audience like it? Will the critics say the band is too old? Happily every tour has been greeted with massive enthusiasm and the passing of the years has if anything made the performances even better.

Once the first few shows are over a routine begins to establish itself. Three shows a week for a few weeks, followed by a week's break, with a longer break perhaps three times a year. At every new city there are press conferences, interviews and 'meet-and-greet' sessions before each show where the local representatives of the record label and city bigwigs will get to meet the band. The entire ensemble of band, entourage, crew, stage and equipment must move on every week or so. The band and entourage have a private jet for the duration of the tour. A fleet of trucks moves the equipment from city to city. Nothing is left to chance. Even electrical generators travel with the crew.

Occasionally, if the next city is not too far away, the band will do a runner, which involves travelling there through the night immediately after the show. It is not popular as every piece of backstage equipment must be packed away and loaded onto trucks after the show, resulting in a late night for everyone.

The logistical command centre is the tour office which is set up in at every venue complete with fax machines, walkie-talkies and computers. Every day the tour office produces a newsletter which is slipped under the door of every member of the entourage. The newsletter details the timetable for the following day which might be a show day, a rest day or a travel day. On show days the band is escorted from the hotel to the venue in the early afternoon in order to perform a sound check. This involves getting on stage and performing parts of a few numbers to ensure that the guys at the mixing board are satisfied with the microphones and speaker levels. Next there may be some press or TV interviews and a meet-and-greet. Often there is time to kill before the show starts. Ronnie and Keith will play a few frames of snooker before moving to the tuning room to run through a few licks. Mick has a warm-up with his personal trainer and Charlie can be seen chatting sociably with anyone on the team.

A feature at every venue is the backstage area. In addition to the dressing rooms for the band and supporting musicians, tour office, wardrobe and make-up, there is the catering department and VIP area. Food and drink is provided on a lavish scale for the entourage and their guests. Hospitality for the guests is on several levels and different passes are provided which allow access to each level. There is the basic hospitality level with beer and snacks, tickets for which are given out by record labels and TV and radio stations. The band will not be seen in this area. Then there is the backstage pass, the demand for which is enormous, particularly in major cities like London,

New York and Los Angeles where the band members have many friends and family. This gives access to a more lavish bar and a wide selection of food. In addition transport is provided from the hotel to the venue for holders of these passes. Finally there is the coveted laminate which gives access to all areas at every show. The laminate is highly sought after and impossible to buy. Only the entourage and very close friends of the band and management will be able to get a laminate.

In 2003 the Rolling Stones celebrated the 40th anniversary of their first public performance. After the appointment of Ronnie Wood in 1978 the line-up had remained unchanged until Bill Wyman's retirement in 1993. One might wonder how a band can stay together for so long without becoming sick of the sight of each other. The Stones have managed it for a number of reasons, not the least of which is that fact that except when working they see little of each other. Even when on tour or in the studio each goes his own way when the day's work is done. At the end of every show, while the audience is shouting for another encore each band member is already in his own blacked-out van leaving the stadium with a few friends and family. Back at the hotel they retire to their respective suites to pass the rest of the night in their own individual way.

The band very nearly broke up in the mid 1980s when Jagger embarked on a solo career. His adviser, Prince Rupert, met with me one day and broke the news in the following way: 'It's rather like a partnership that has been together for a long time. One day a partner decides he wants to leave the partnership to follow his own pursuits. Well, that time has come and Mick has decided to make some solo albums.'

Shortly afterwards it was announced that Mick had signed a huge recording contract with CBS. If that solo career had taken off, in all probability it would have meant the end of the

Stones. But Mick's solo albums were unsuccessful, in spite of large sums spent on promotion and music videos, and his projected solo tour was cancelled.

Just how close the Stones came to breaking up is evidenced by the fact that there was no Stones tour between the years 1981 and 1989. In earlier years every new studio album released by the Stones was followed by a lengthy tour. Although an album was released in 1986 there was no tour to promote it because Mick was busy with his solo projects. This caused a rift in the band, particularly between Mick and Keith, which took years to heal. Other band members had released solo albums over the years, but these were low-budget niche projects for which there was only a small market. Mick's multi-million dollar deal was intended to launch a solo career which would be big enough to rival the Stones.

The Stones were contractually obligated to record and deliver a final studio album to Atlantic Records. The album was made at Olympia Studios in Paris over a period of many months in 1985. During the recording sessions the tension between Mick and the others reached its peak when Mick put promotional activities for his own album before his obligations to the Stones. There was evidence of this when I was invited by Ronnie to visit the studios during a recording session. Mick arrived late and in a very ill humour. He immediately cleared the studio of everyone but the band and told Ronnie to get his manager and manageress (meaning me and my girlfriend) out of the studio, together with the other guests.

Charlie Watts was normally a quiet and reserved individual, but later that evening, as I learned from Ronnie, when it became clear that Mick was more interested in his solo album than the Stones project, Charlie became so incensed with Mick's conduct that he punched him hard enough to knock him to the ground. For several years after that album was completed Mick and Keith had no further contact with each other. It was only the good work of Ronnie acting as go-between that eventually brought them together again.

Another cause for tension within the band has been Ronnie's and Keith's addictions to drugs and alcohol. Mick has been clean for many years and rarely drinks even a glass of wine when on tour. Ronnie and Keith, on the other hand, were permanently fuelled by a combination of cocaine and alcohol and this has at times affected their playing ability.

I remember taking Ronnie to David Forecast, a Harley Street doctor, for his compulsory pre-tour medical. He asked Ronnie how many units of alcohol he consumed on a regular basis. Ronnie started totting up, starting with the draught Guinness at the beginning of the day and finishing up with late-night vodkas. The doctor looked at the numbers and commented: 'Hm, not too bad. As far as the insurance company is concerned it's almost within the acceptable number of units per week.'

'Per week?' said Ronnie. 'What are you talking about? That's my daily intake.' This reply meant he failed the medical and we had to start again with another doctor. Ronnie's addiction became so severe that he was unable to pass the insurance medical for the 2002/3 tour and had to spend a month drying out in a clinic in Arizona before he was in a fit state to tour again. It should be said that he completed the tour without either drugs or alcohol, leaving Keith as the only band member who continued to use both.

Of course there is a huge financial incentive for the Stones to keep touring. Profits from the shows, which are invariably sold out, run into hundreds of millions of dollars. In common with any well-managed company the Stones keep their tax liabilities to a minimum. Surprising as it may seem, virtually no UK tax is payable on the huge profits that the tours generate. Even though the band members have homes in the UK and some of them are UK residents, their foreign tour profits are tax-free thanks to a legal loophole which allows UK residents engaged in foreign employment to bring their earnings into the UK free of tax. Before every tour a foreign employer engages the band's exclusive overseas services for an agreed remuneration in order to gain UK tax-exempt status. Of course tax is payable on the profits from shows performed in the UK, but in some mysterious way UK shows never seem to produce much profit as the expenses are so high. It was part of my job to review the contracts on Ronnie's behalf. I can't speak for other band members, but certainly the tax scheme worked perfectly for him. It was audited more than once by both the US tax authorities and the UK Inland Revenue.

In order to further mitigate the tax bite, albums are recorded overseas in France or the Caribbean for delivery to foreign record labels. The band is fortunate in having Mick Jagger, a graduate of the London School of Economics, keeping an eye on the finances. When Mick was knighted in 2002 for services to popular music, it crossed my mind to wonder if the citation should more appropriately have been for services to tax avoidance – all of it entirely legal, of course.

To understand the financial conflicts between band members, it may help to have the workings of the music industry briefly explained. Every record sold or played on the radio generates several revenue streams, including one for the performers and a separate one for the writers of the material. In the case of the Stones, the songwriters are nearly always Mick and Keith, though occasionally the band has covered a song written by a third party, Bob Dylan for example. In addition Mick and Keith (as the Glimmer Twins) take producer royalties from record sales. Additional publishing and song-writing royalties arise from radio play, performance revenue and commercials, as when Microsoft used 'Start Me Up' for the launch of a new version of Windows. The catalogue of Stones songs owned by Jagger and Richards is a priceless asset which will go on producing revenue long after the band has ceased to record and perform.

None of this would be a problem were it not for the fact that all the costs of making the record, as well as many promotional expenses such as the cost of making music videos, are set against the revenues of the performers. The songwriters, by contrast, receive their revenues from the first record sold regardless of the costs of production. The Stones have a history of spending excessive sums recording an album, to the extent that nearly all the royalties from sales of the finished product are eaten up by the costs. The end result is that Mick and Keith enjoy a very substantial income from their song-writing, while the other band members receive relatively little from album sales and have to rely on tour profits for most of their income.

At the point where I met Ronnie, just before the start of the 'Tattoo You' tour in 1981 (Bill's penultimate tour), Ronnie was being paid a weekly wage. When I first raised this question with Prince Rupert Loewenstein, the Stones' financial adviser, and proposed that Ronnie should receive a share of profits, he argued that profit sharers must also take their share of any losses and Ronnie wasn't in a position to bear these risks. To me this was a neat argument, but a purely theoretical one, devised to deny Ronnie his rightful financial place in the band. Fortunately, before the start of the next tour, 'Steel Wheels', I was able to negotiate a profit-sharing contract which increased in percentage value over the years until it was only a little smaller than an equal share.

A further huge contribution to the revenues comes from tour merchandise. Every venue has numerous outlets selling T-shirts, jackets, sweats, and other items decorated with the

Stones logo. New designs are produced for every tour. Merchandise sales add more than 20 percent to the revenues derived from ticket sales. The mark-up on merchandise, as one would expect, is enormous. While he remained a member of the Rolling Stones, Bill Wyman was one of the equal owners of the Stones name and logo – a valuable resource in its own right. When he resigned in 1993 the remaining original members had to pay him off. The deal was for them to pay him a percentage of the next tour, even though he didn't perform, in return for which they acquired his share of the Stones name.

The budget of a Stones tour is larger than that of a major movie and the reliable and consistent revenue stream it generates would be the envy of any movie company. As it runs along the same tried and tested path that it has covered for four decades, the organisation ticks along like a well-oiled machine. No band has ever put bums on seats like the Stones.

12

Letter to Ronnie Wood

Dear Ronnie – I recently finished reading your biography, *Ronnie*. My name is mentioned several times and in every instance you have something negative to say about me. Whilst I accept your criticism for any mistakes I made during the twenty or so years I was looking after your interests, I am disappointed that you have given me no credit on the plus side for the many things that went well. It may be that you are suffering from amnesia or that your self-admitted addictions have clouded your memory, so I thought I would take this opportunity to balance the books, as it were, and set the record straight.

When we first met in Philadelphia in 1979 at the start of the 'Tattoo You' Stones tour your finances were not in great shape, to say the least. You were receiving foreclosure notices for non-payment of the mortgage on your house in Los Angeles, you had spent the last of your money supporting the New Barbarians tour, you had sold your rights to royalties on the Stones album *Emotional Rescue*, you had received and spent a substantial advance for your song-writing, you had large outstanding bills to the attorney who had been handling your affairs, you had failed to file any tax returns for several years and drug dealers were harassing you for payment. You were a Rolling Stone in name only and had contracted to go on tour for a weekly wage without any right to a share of the tour profits.

I can honestly say that if I had known the disastrous state you had got yourself into I would not have taken you on as a client. It took me years to sort out the mess, putting in thousands of hours without pay. By the time we parted company several Stones' tours later I had negotiated a profit share for you very close to an equal share with the three remaining band members.

It must have slipped your memory that I got your art career off the ground by arranging for you to go to the studio in San Francisco and then putting on your first exhibitions in the US. Over the years I arranged and attended dozens of your art shows all over the world. We also went on several art tours together, to Japan for two weeks and around the US. The sales from these tours enabled you to maintain a more than comfortable lifestyle during the long period when there were no Stones' tours. When Lord Lloyd Webber became your patron after seeing your work in my gallery, you had a solid base of collectors around the world and were poised for take-off. Phil Carson and I started the company which published and distributed your limited editions and when you fired him at your wife's insistence I had to buy out his share of the company.

To say that I put you on a budget of $200 per week in New York must be a typographical error – surely there is a zero missing. For starters you had a full time housekeeper, then there were limos at your beck and call, designer clothes and expensive holidays, plus the cost of feeding your addiction which alone was more than $200 per week.

You are critical of Woody's on the Beach, saying that although you had good times there it was 'pricy' and a 'fiasco'. In fact it cost you nothing. It was financed by investor friends of David Giles. You and your family had a couple of all-expenses-paid trips to Miami each year to be at Woody's and it was a permanent exhibition for your artwork as well as a showcase for some of your favourite old musicians who performed there. In fact it was closed by the Mayor of South Beach because it was so successful – the crowds leaving the club in the early hours of the morning made so much noise that the local residents petitioned the Mayor to have its licence withdrawn.

Buying a home in Ireland in 1980 was a life-changing move for the better in your life, yet I could not see my name anywhere in your chapter about Sandymount, your estate in Ireland. Just for the record, I invited you to stay with my great friend Denny Cordell in Ireland not for tax reasons, as you claim – actually Irish tax residency would have been a disaster for you as it would have meant paying huge taxes on your tour earnings – but because I thought you would enjoy Ireland. As you know, I regard it as my home country and it is where my parents lived and died. I introduced you to Sandymount and arranged a private sale to you from my old school chum Jonathan Irwin. Perhaps you have forgotten that when you bought the property it came with only a few acres. I spent the next three years having tea with the neighbouring farmer (one of the few Irishmen who has foresworn alcohol) before I could persuade him to sell you a further sixty acres of land surrounding your house. It was this extra land that has made Sandymount one of the most valuable small estates in County Kildare.

Perhaps I should have taken greater notice when your wife built a pool house at Sandymount larger and more expensive than the house itself. It was an early warning of the extravagances that were the downfall of the Harrington Club.

You mention that you did phenomenally well with some Sky shares you bought. True, you made a gain of several million pounds, but you have obviously forgotten where the shares came from. You did not buy them. I allotted you some shares in my company Sports Internet Group at the founders' price of 25p. Two years later the company was taken over by Sky. You got £6.50 of Sky shares for every 25p share – a 25–1 winner!

If the Harrington Club had been able to open within its

budget of £2 million the loss would have been more than covered by the Sky profit. Once your wife took control of the design and décor the budget flew out the window and the ultimate loss was far greater than it should have been. Every time I or the architect tried to reign her in her reply was the same, 'It's our money and we can do what we like with it.' Of course I'm sorry that we went into this ill-fated venture – after all, I lost more than a million pounds of my own money trying to keep the Harrington going. But to say you lost everything as a result is something of an exaggeration. Your wife's extravagance (with an American Express bill of up to £100,000 a month, the £1,000 a week on flowers mentioned in your book is the least of it) plus your own generous nature were contributory factors to your financial situation. You bought houses for your brothers, supported your wife's family, poured hundreds of thousand of pounds into improvements to Holmwood, your London house, and lent money to people who were never going to be able to repay it.

Imagine my surprise when I heard that the word on the tour was that you had to pay me a seven-figure sum to get rid of me. Although I am not at liberty to reveal the actual sum agreed with Jamie, you and I know it was a fraction of the money that I put into the Harrington from my own resources and a tiny percentage of the tour profits you received in the following years.

It is sad to think that time and the Harrington appear to have erased from your memory the better things we did together and the thousands of hours spent on the road, in the studio, at the races and having fun in Ireland.

Perhaps a fairer summing-up is provided by your own words, taken from your art book *Every Picture Tells a Story*, published in 1998: 'This book is dedicated to Nick Cowan for the stability, income and friendship he brought me.'

13

Jerry Lee Lewis, Chuck Berry, Bobby Womack

An example of the spirit of rock 'n' roll at its best was the time Ronnie and I went down to Memphis to make a video with Jerry Lee Lewis. If the Rolling Stones ever worry about getting old they only have to think about Jerry Lee and Chuck Berry, two of the original legends of rock 'n' roll, who are still going strong.

Immortalised by Chuck Berry in his 'Long-distance inform-ation, get me Memphis Tennessee', Memphis was at one time home to the three kings of Rock, Country and the Blues – Elvis, Johnny Cash and B. B. King. All recorded at Sun Studios, where a parade of legendary rockers cut their first tracks. For me the greatest of them all is Jerry Lee Lewis who, having gone through six wives and a lifetime of problems with alcohol and drug addiction, still managed to release a new album in 2007, called appropriately enough 'Last Man Standing'. The biggest musical disappointment of my youth was the cancellation of Jerry Lee's tour of the UK in 1958 when it was discovered he had married his thirteen-year-old cousin.

When the opportunity arose for me to meet my idol in Memphis in 1986 I was thrilled. Sun Studios' producer, Chips Moman, contacted my office to see if Ronnie Wood could come to Memphis for a few days to take part in a music video with Jerry Lee and Carl Perkins to promote a new album they were making with Johnny Cash and Roy Orbison. It was a rush

ick Cowan at
on, 1960

avid Jacobs,
licitor, 1967

Nigel Dempster

Nick's $1.6m is just the ticket

THE biggest racing jackpot in the history of the turf — an astonishing $1,600,000 — has been scooped in California by leading West End art dealer Anthony Speelman, 46, and his pal, Old Etonian solicitor Nick Cowan, 44.

The two — neither of whom bets regularly — haven't stopped celebrating since their day out at Santa Anita racecourse, California, eight days ago when they each placed a modest $64 on a nine horse accumulator.

For divorcee Cowan — who has lived in Los Angeles for ten years, latterly as a showbusiness manager — it is a double celebration. He had just announced his decision to marry the girl he has been living with for the past seven years, stunning dress designer Julie Styne, 26 — granddaughter of lyricist Jule Styne who wrote Funny Girl and Three Coins in the Fountain.

Jubilantly Cowan tells me: 'It was complete freak. Firstly, I don't often go to the races and secondly, the jackpot has built up over 24 days, which is unheard of. My feet haven't touched the ground since it happened!'

It was the last day of the racing season on the course; and the rules are that the jackpot has to be won. To his profound disbelief Cowan found he held the winning ticket with the first seven out of the nine winners. 'I already agreed with Anthony that in the unlikely event of either of us winning, we would share the proceeds — but of course we never for one moment thought we would.'

Speelman, also divorced and an Old Harrovian, runs his family's art gallery in Piccadilly and has known Cowan since their schooldays. A keen sportsman — he plays golf and cricket and shoots — Speelman is the part-owner of the hugely successful racehorse Zoffany, which was due to have its last outing before going to stud in Australia. 'We were only there to watch Zoffany for the last time and ironically, in the end it was decided not to run him' adds Cowan.

Speelman was flying home from California last night $800,000 richer and from Switzerland, where his parents now live, his mother tells me: 'He telephoned us immediately. We could hardly believe it, because although Anthony does have a share in one or two racehorses, he actually doesn't bet a lot at all.

Nick and Julie: Two reasons for celebrating   Picture Paul Harris

Nigel Dempster's Diary in the *Daily Mail*, Tuesday, April 28, 1987

ick Cowan with Nigel Dempster

cartoon strip based on the *Guinness Book of Records*

Factfile FROM THE GUINNESS BOOK OF RECORDS

E WORLD'S
RGEST
OKMAKER

DBROKES
TH A
RNOVER
OM
AMBLING
1986 OF
40
LLION.
EY ALSO
D 1660
TTING
OPS IN THE
ITED
GDOM
THE END
986, AS
LL AS
O IN
LGIUM.

NICHOLAS JOHN COWAN, ALONG WITH
FELLOW BRITON ANTHONY A.
SPEELMAN, WON $1,627,084.40,
AFTER TAX,
ON A $64
NINE HORSE
ACCUMULATOR
AT SANTA
ANITA
RACECOURSE,
CALIFORNIA,
USA ON 19
APRIL 1987.
THEIR FIRST
SEVEN
SELECTIONS
WON AND
THE PAYOUT
WAS FOR A
JACKPOT,
ACCUMULATED
OVER 24
DAYS.

Drawn by DICK MILLINGTON

THE ONLY RECORDED INSTANCE OF
A RACING CORRESPONDENT
FORECASTING TEN OUT OF TEN
WINNERS ON RACE CARD WAS AT
DELAWARE PARK, DELAWARE,
USA, ON 28 JULY 1974 BY CHARLES
LAMB OF THE *BALTIMORE NEWS
AMERICAN*.

Jerry Lee Lewis, Jerry Lee's guest, Nick Cowan, Jo and Ronnie Wood,
Memphis 1988

nnie, Jo, Nick Cowan and Julie his wife, Madrid 1992

Arriving in Japan, 1993 for an exhibition of Ronnie's paintings

The president of the Rolling Stones Fan Club, Ronnie and the author made up as a geisha

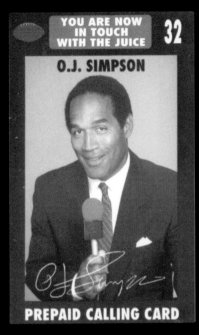

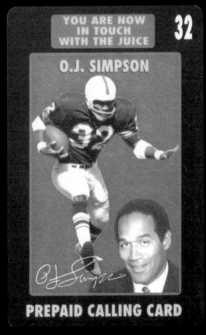

O. J. Simpson phone cards, 1995

Bobby Keys with Nick Cowan
in 1997

Ronnie and Nick Cowan on
tour 1997

job as they had only three days to record the album and one to shoot the video. Ronnie jumped at the chance to work with some of his legendary heroes and we set off from New York to Memphis, where we checked into the Peabody Hotel. The Peabody is celebrated for its flock of ducks which spend the day in the pool on the roof of the hotel and twice a day march across the hotel lobby, where a red carpet has been unrolled for them, to and from their sleeping quarters. On arrival we made contact with Jerry Lee, who invited us over to his house for some beers before going out on the town for the evening.

The house was not much different from a million other suburban American homes, except for the fact that the entire ground-floor carpeting and furniture were encased in a clear plastic see-through covering. This was no flimsy dust-sheet of the type thrown over furniture by decorators; it was heavy-duty transparent plastic which was firmly fixed over the flooring and completely covered the sofas and other chairs in the sitting room. Thinking of Jerry Lee's fierce reputation as a hell-raiser and his nickname 'Killer', I assumed the purpose was that a bloodbath could take place in the room which could then be hosed down to leave no trace of the event.

I had anticipated a thrill on being in the presence of a Very Dangerous Person, but have to admit a degree of disappointment when Jerry Lee let us into his house. He greeted us affably, went to the kitchen to get a few beers, sat down in his plastic-covered armchair and lit his pipe. He was wearing a beige woolly cardigan and brown trousers and looked like everybody's favourite uncle. A pair of slippers would have completed the picture of domestic normality. The only evidence of the Killer that I saw came when Jerry Lee pointed out a couple of bullet holes in the wall high up above the stairs which he said had been made during a fight with one of his wives. Just who had fired the shots seemed to have slipped his memory. Things livened up later that evening after dinner when at a small club in downtown Memphis Jerry Lee and Ronnie jumped on stage and joined the band for a lively rendition of 'Great Balls Of Fire'. It was a more sedate Jerry Lee who sat on the piano stool rather the piano pumping wild man of his youth who would kick the stool across the stage. After a cheery 'See you in the morning', Jerry Lee went home. We had a few drinks at a Memphis bar and retired to the Peabody somewhat the worse for wear. The video shoot was scheduled to start the next morning and we had an 8.00 a.m. call. In common with many rockers, Ronnie is a night person and the only way to be sure to get him on parade for an 8.00 a.m. start is to stay up all night with him. An essential ingredient of these all-night sessions is loud, repetitive music in competition with the TV. We were interrupted several times during the night by the hotel manager complaining that some of the guests were unreasonable enough to want to sleep.

Having managed a video production company in New York in the early '80s, I was well aware of what was involved in shooting a music video. The director would submit a concept to the artist and record label and a budget would be agreed with the production company. The cost of the shoot depended largely on the location and the number of days filming involved. Even the lowest-budget video of a band on-stage employed several cameramen, a steadycam and an array of lights, but the Memphis video turned out to be quite a different animal. The budget was little more than that of a home movie. It was to be a one-day, one-camera shoot on the streets of Memphis and the only prop was an ancient Oldsmobile convertible in which Jerry Lee, Ronnie and Carl Perkins were to drive around. Carl was to be at the wheel since it was his track that the video was promoting.

At the appointed hour we met at the starting point of the

drive-around and went into the trailer where the make-up girl was waiting. Jerry Lee was dressed to kill in his best stage clothes and had liberally doused himself in a powerfully scented aftershave. 'Hey, Jerry Lee, you smell good! What you got on?' said the cheery young make-up girl. 'I got a hard on, honey, but I didn't know you could smell it,' came Jerry Lee's instant reply. Carl Perkins had some trouble with his hairpiece, afraid that it would blow off during the ride in the convertible. It was decided that many of the shots would be stationary in front of Memphis landmarks such as the gates of Graceland, Beale Street (of Blues fame) and Sun Studios. In order to deal with the problem of Carl's hairpiece the moving shots were to be filmed at low speed and speeded up in the edit room later. By late afternoon everyone had had enough and the director called a wrap. It was hot and humid and we stopped for a beer and burgers.

There are several claimants in Memphis for the title of Elvis's favourite burger joint, but Jerry Lee assured that he would take us to the real thing. The burgers on offer go some way to explaining Elvis's huge weight gain. Not only were they of the highest fat content allowable by law under the description of ground beef, but they were deep-fried in a vat of rendered beef dripping. It was explained to us that the unique flavour of the burgers was obtained by the continuous use of the same frying medium. The vat had not been emptied in years and was continually replenished by the fat melting from the frying burgers. Luckily we didn't know this until after we had hungrily eaten them, or we might not have been able to stomach them so readily. This meal was washed down by a few more beers which put an end to the long day's proceedings. Having missed a night's sleep all we wanted to do was to retire to the Peabody for a rest. We said our goodbyes to Jerry Lee but I was to see him again not long afterwards at our live music venue in South Beach, Miami, which opened in 1987.

Another legend I met on my rock 'n' roll travels was Chuck Berry. He was a lot less fun than Jerry Lee, it has to be said, because of the huge chip he carries around on his shoulder. Sometimes known as the father of rock 'n' roll, he is still performing in his eighties and both he and Jerry Lee were among the original inductees of the Rock 'n' Roll Hall of Fame when it was set up in 1986. Several gaol terms in Chuck's career have embittered him. Notoriously difficult to satisfy, he takes it out on promoters who don't read the small print in the rider to his contract carefully enough. This rider specifies in the greatest detail the exact requirements of the dressing area, food, drink, towels and accessories that are to be provided for Chuck. The towels are to be of a certain size, the dressing room a set distance from the stage, the refreshments at a certain temperature and so on. There are set financial penalties for any failure to provide the exact requirements laid down in the rider.

On arrival at a venue Chuck sets about checking that the distances, sizes and other details are all present and correct. Any failure will have to be paid for in cash before he will go on stage. On one occasion in California at a show in Irvine Meadows that I was co-promoting I was foolish enough to ask him if there was anything else he wanted, as he seemed to be satisfied with the backstage arrangements. 'Yeah,' he said. 'Get me some white pussy after the show.'

Chuck often travelled from venue to venue without a band. He would expect a band to be provided that had been rehearsed in every song he had ever written. He would not provide a set list to let them know what numbers were going to be played on that particular night. He'd just play a chord or two of a song and expect the band to come straight in with the right key. Many of his live performances, including the show at Irvine Meadows, were marred by this unnecessary obstacle. The chip on his shoulder does the great man no favours.

Another huge talent with a similar chip is Bobby Womack. In his case, though, it has held him back significantly, and may have prevented him from being inducted into the Rock 'n' Roll Hall of Fame. He might well be thought fit company to be numbered with the legends above were it not for an attitude that has made him all but impossible to work with.

It was while the Woods were living in Wimbledon that Ronnie introduced me to Bobby Womack, whom I was later to manage for a couple of years in the '90s. He was a hugely talented singer/songwriter and musician. His music came under the categories of Soul and R & B and he had many hits on the R & B charts. However, he became embittered with the music industry because he was never able to cross over and achieve real success in the pop/rock mainstream charts. He allowed this resentment to become so powerful that he became a very troublesome customer to deal with and it was only with difficulty that I was able to secure a record deal for him.

As a young man of twenty Bobby had composed 'It's All Over Now', which was one of the Stones' first hit singles, but his conduct alienated Mick Jagger, who once asked me what I was doing with 'that awful person' when he saw me backstage at a Stones concert with Bobby. Keith and Ronnie on the other hand had the greatest respect for Bobby's musical talent. Ronnie had a recording studio in Wimbledon at the bottom of his garden with a flat above, where Bobby came to stay while he worked on some songs with Ronnie. Typically, this ended in trouble. Keith had given Bobby a present of a custom-made gold bracelet which he wore all the time. One night while staying in Wimbledon Bobby entertained a girl in the flat, and in the morning both girl and bracelet were gone. Bobby was deeply upset by this theft and quite inexplicably held Ronnie to blame for the fact that he'd lost his bracelet.

Bobby had been a visitor to my house in Beverly Hills on the several occasions that Ronnie had been to stay with me. In 1983 I formed a relationship with a new record label, Continuum in New Jersey, which was run by a young Englishman with more money than sense. By then Bobby had run the gamut of record labels including United Artists, Arista, Columbia, MCA and Beverly Glen with whom he had his greatest success with his album 'The Poet'. None of these labels were prepared to work with Bobby again in spite of his undoubted talent. He was just too difficult. I persuaded Continuum to give Bobby a recording contract and he went to work in a studio in Los Angeles.

Time went by and we were soon into overtime, having exceeded the budget allowed for recording. Bobby regarded this as standard practice and was insulted that a label would expect an artist to stay within budget. I managed to get Rod Stewart, whom I knew socially, to sing on one of Bobby's tracks and eventually the album was delivered for release in 1994 with the title *Resurrection* – aptly bestowed, as Bobby was making a comeback. In order to promote the album Bobby went on a tour of selected cities to be interviewed on local radio. The problem I had was that Bobby wasn't interested in the constraints of the promotional budget. There was no way he would go to a radio station unless a stretch limo was provided to collect him from his hotel.

When he went to New Orleans it was at a time when I needed to be elsewhere, so I made arrangements for a limo to pick Bobby up as usual. When the interview was over he proceeded to disappear for two days, taking the limo with him. This was being charged to my American Express card, so the limo driver was in no way concerned that the meter was kept running for 48 hours. That was the problem with Bobby – if he could get away with it he would.

The album was only a modest success, and of course in Bobby's mind it was entirely the fault of the record label that it had not gone straight into the charts. Bobby flew to New Jersey and stormed in to Continuum's offices where he demanded the return of his master tapes. Violence was threatened and my relationship with the label was irreparably damaged. A year later Continuum went out of business after losing many millions of dollars. My relationship with Bobby had cost me a small fortune since I suffered the cost of the budget over-runs and he never paid me a cent in commission. It is hard not to admire him as a talent, but one can only say of Bobby that he was his own worst enemy.

14

New York Diary

It is 1984 and Ed Koch has been Mayor of New York for eight years. The Mayor and his Council have just voted themselves a hefty pay rise in spite of the fact that New York City is plagued by crime and strikes and is financially unstable. At the press conference announcing the rises the Mayor is asked if the pay hikes will bring about an improvement in conditions in the City. The Mayor replies, 'It's like chicken soup – it may not do any good but it certainly won't do any harm.'

The landlord of my apartment has decided to redevelop the property and the tenants including me are given notice to quit. I have been allowing a lady realtor to work out of my offices for a few months and she brings to my attention the rent control laws in New York which are very stringent. Many buildings are occupied by tenants paying rents which are a fraction of the market value. These tenants have a legal right to remain in place for the rest of their lives with only minimal cost of living increases in the rents. The realtor has found a double-fronted brownstone on 71st Street opposite the Frick Museum which can be purchased at a knockdown price because it is partially occupied by rent-controlled tenants. I manage to round up a few investors including Denny Cordell and we buy the building.

A few houses away from 5th Avenue, the brownstone was once an elegant mansion built for a railroad tycoon. It is reputed to have been a speakeasy in the days of Prohibition. The building was long ago divided up into separate apartments, though it retains a mahogany-panelled library on the first floor that becomes my office. There are two apartments on each of five floors and two single-floor apartments, a total of twelve of which five are occupied by rent-controlled tenants. Of course the building would be worth considerably more if it were vacant. I start negotiations with each of the tenants but they are asking far too much to move out and I decide to leave things as they are for the time being. A more pressing problem is a plague of pigeons, which are nesting on every ledge. The mess and noise are unbearable.

I arrange a meeting with a pigeon control expert I find in the Yellow Pages. We meet on the roof of the building where he spreads handfuls of birdseed for the pigeons. He tells me it is 'wacky' seed, explaining that when the pigeons eat it they fly erratically for a few minutes before crashing to their deaths. The seed has been impregnated with strychnine, a deadly poison. Later I learn that this process, although effective, is highly illegal and when the pigeon man tells me that he knows a 'winkler' who can help persuade the rent-controlled tenants to leave, I have to decline his offer.

In buying the building I have some temporary financing from the vendor which must be replaced with a mortgage. My friend the realtor has a connection with the First Women's Bank of New York and the manager comes round to inspect the property. The manager is an attractive lady in her thirties who, after being shown round the building, asks if she can go round on her own. When I go to look for her I'm rather surprised to find her in my bed. What's a man supposed to do if he wants to get a mortgage? There seems no alternative to joining her. New York seems to be sex-obsessed. Plato's Retreat is advertising for swingers, the 'Ugly George' show is on television nightly, in which George walks the streets with a camera and persuades single girls to come back to the studio to strip for him. A year or two later AIDS makes its appearance and suddenly everything changes.

One of the tenants is a three-martini lunch man who comes rolling back every afternoon in time to persecute the dog-walkers on their rounds from 5th Avenue. He is armed with toy bombs from FAO Schwartz which he drops from his fourth-floor window into the midst of a group of dogs. The resulting explosion causes chaos as the dogs try to run off in all directions, leaving the long-suffering dog-walker tied up in a tangle of leashes. Luckily the tenant moves away after a year, deciding that the climate in Miami suits him better. There are four remaining rent-controlled tenants.

In the meantime I have formed an alliance with a London-based video production company and a US branch is established in the basement of the building. MTV is becoming all-powerful in the music business and every artist must have a music video to promote a new album. We have two award-winning directors based in New York and are producing music videos for some big-time rock bands. Often they have to be delivered to a dead-line which involves the production crew working through the night. Loud music gets played, much to the annoyance of the tenants, and the crew are careless about leaving the elevator doors open, so those living at the top of the building have to walk down to the basement to catch the elevator. It seems like a good time to talk to the tenants again about vacating the building.

On the night of the Super Bowl in 1986, a freezing cold night in New York, I am watching the game with a group of friends when we hear fire sirens in the street. The fire engines are right outside the building. The doorbell rings and I let in the firemen who charge up the stairs to the top floor, dragging fire hoses behind them. One of the apartments on the top floor is on fire. Within minutes the fire is extinguished, but not before hundreds of gallons of water have cascaded down the central stairwell. It is so cold with the front door open that great icicles have formed on the staircase. The cause of the fire is unknown. I suspect the tenant fell asleep smoking in bed. In any event the apartment is uninhabitable and there is one less tenant to deal with.

Eventually I agree terms for the other tenants to vacate and the building is put on the market. By the time the tenants and the mortgage have been paid off there is a decent profit to come from the sale and I'm ready to move.

After ten or so years training horses in Ireland Denny Cordell had had enough and decided to come back into the music business. He rejoined Island Records and from around 1991 had the job of running their operations in New York. Among various acts that he signed for the company in that period were the Irish band the Cranberries, who went on to sell millions of albums. Thanks to a royalty deal I negotiated for him, he was soon in a position to gain independence from Island, and in 1994 was ready to launch a new record label of his own, backed by millions of dollars of funding from the German recording giant BMG. The offices were to be in Dublin and everything was on track for the new label. The aim was that I would act as business manager while his son Barney would also play a pivotal role. In December of that year DC came to stay with me for a week in Beverly Hills. We were out on the town every night toasting the future success of the new label with rather too many bottles of fine Bordeaux.

January came around. I had a telephone call from Denny saying he was feeling the effects of too much partying but I did not think anything of it at the time. Towards the end of the month I heard from Barney that his dad was feeling so rotten that he had gone into hospital in Dublin with what he thought was hepatitis. I had arranged an exhibition of Ronnie Wood's art in Buenos Aires to coincide with the arrival of the Stones tour in Argentina. In Buenos Aires I checked into the hotel where the Stones were staying, which was besieged night and day by fanatical fans desperate to catch a glimpse of their heroes. By now I was getting regular bulletins on Denny's illness. At times he seemed to be recovering, only to have a relapse days later. After a few days a call came from Barney saying that DC was very sick and wanted to see me as soon as possible.

I flew over immediately. When I got to the hospital I was dismayed to find Denny connected up to an array of drips and drains. With an oxygen feed in his nostrils and a mask over his mouth it was difficult to understand what he was trying to say. By then he had been diagnosed with lymphoma and treated with a massive dose of chemotherapy. He was too ill for any visits from his friends and for several days and nights Barney and I together with Denny's mother Mary took shifts around the clock keeping a vigil in his room. For three days there was little improvement and he was so weak he could hardly speak. On about the fourth day I was on the morning shift when Denny suddenly sat up in bed, took the mask off his mouth and in the clearest and most lucid voice summoned the nurse: 'This is Nick, my lawyer and my friend. I am going home with him today.'

Of course the doctors would not allow him to leave then and there but it did appear that he was making an amazing recovery, so much so that for the first time in a week Barney, Mary and I went into Dublin and had dinner in a restaurant with his family and close friends. We had not finished dinner when the hospital called. Denny had relapsed into a coma from which he never awoke. He died three days later on 18 February.

DC was only fifty-one when he died. He had crammed

those years full with wine, women, song, the arts, animals, children, and every sensory experience available to man.

I stayed with the family at Denny's house in County Carlow until the funeral a week later. On a typically grey and rainy Irish day the hundreds of mourners trudged their way from the house to the local church two miles away, following an ancient hearse drawn by two black-plumed horses. During the funeral service I couldn't hold back the tears at saying goodbye to my closest friend, someone I had been in constant touch with for the past twenty years. We had gone through good, bad, funny and exciting times together. Hard to believe I would never see him again. DC was buried with his racing colours, and the eminent Irish author J. P. Donleavy wrote an epitaph headed 'He died with his boots on'.

After the interment a stupendous Irish wake was held at Denny's favourite pub, O'Shea's in the village of Borris. This was no ordinary pub. Hammers, mousetraps and wellington boots hung from the ceiling just above the bacon slicer and the sides of ham. A customer might be ordering a pint of Guinness and a cheese roll, together with half a pound of galvanised nails. In the back room where the music was blaring, family and friends from all walks of life danced and drank the night away. As the night drew to a close and the music slowed, an old boy who for years had helped Denny with the horses put his arm round my shoulder.

'Nick,' said he in his heavy Irish brogue, 'We shurely planted him roight, we shurely did.'

15

Guinness Book of Records

This is the story of a bet that made it into the *Guinness Book of World Records*, but it is also the story of a horse called Zoffany, who was due to make his final appearance on Easter Sunday 1987 in the Grade One San Juan Capistrano.

Zoffany belonged to Anthony Speelman, a friend of mine from England. He had been shipped to California at the end of his three-year-old career in England and had gradually established himself as the top grass horse on the West Coast. Trained by John Gosden, Zoffany had his first Graded Stakes win in the Citation Handicap at Hollywood Park in 1985. I went to the races that day with Charles Benson, who was in Los Angeles for his regular winter visit. Charles, a friend from London, was a compulsive gambler, had been for many years racing correspondent for the *Daily Express* and liked nothing more than betting on American football, but despite his vast knowledge of the subject, which he would gladly share with anyone prepared to listen, results almost invariably went against him. So it was with a depleted bankroll that Charles headed for Hollywood Park with me for company.

The fairy story began there. Zoffany nosed ahead in the final furlong to beat the Charlie Whittingham-trained favourite Lord of War at the rewarding odds of just over 6–1. Gosden announced that Zoffany's next race would be the Hollywood Turf Cup, a $500,000 Grade One, over a mile and a half, a race that would attract entries not only from the East Coast but also from Europe.

Anthony flew in to LA for the weekend of the race and a bunch of us assembled for dinner at my favourite restaurant, Le Dome on Sunset Boulevard. It was a stellar field for the race that included winners of the Washington International, the Man of War Stakes and a French-trained hot-shot owned by Suzy Volterra. Zoffany's chances were assessed by the racing press as somewhere between 16– and 22–1. It was a chilly day as Anthony and I set off for Hollywood Park but we felt no chill when Zoffany brilliantly ridden by Eddie Delahoussaye pounced on the pace-setting Vanlandingham and ran clear away to win by 2½ lengths, confounding the sceptics at odds of 23–1. I left Hollywood Park with more cash than I have ever had on me leaving a racecourse and with a fierce determination to follow Zoffany throughout his career.

Zoffany continued on an upward trend, winning the Sunset Handicap on Independence Day the following year, and although he was injured in the Arlington Million he came back to defeat the mighty Ferdinand, winner of the Kentucky Derby, in the San Luis Rey Stakes. By now, Anthony had sold a controlling interest in the horse to Segenhoe Stud in Australia, where he would stand as a stallion, and it was decided the San Juan Capistrano would be his last race.

Zoffany by now was a seven-year-old, holder of two course records at Hollywood Park, but the years of training and racing on lightning fast surfaces had begun to take their toll and Gosden decided that it would be an unacceptable risk to the horse's fragile legs to let him take part in the big race on Easter Sunday. I was in Europe at the time skiing in Verbier but had already booked my flight back to LA to make sure I was there, not only for the race but for the whole build-up to Santa Anita's biggest weekend of the year.

Anthony was due to fly in on the Friday before the race and although he had known the week before that Zoffany would not take part, he decided to come anyway to see his teenage daughter who lived in LA. As usual we met for dinner on the Friday night at Le Dome to discuss the forthcoming races. Although it was rather depressing to see Zoffany's old rivals, all of whom he had beaten in previous races, contesting the big prize, a little spice was added to our discussions as there was a huge Pick Nine Jackpot Pool up for grabs.

The Pick Nine is what is known as an exotic wager. There are nine races a day at Santa Anita and to win the jackpot you must literally find all nine winners. A line with one horse in each race will cost $2, but if you want to put in multiple choices the sum staked will quickly climb. For instance, a ticket with one selection in four races and two in the other five will cost $32. The more choices you make the more it costs and if no one is successful in selecting all nine winners the pool carries over.

As luck would have it, no one had won the Pick Nine for 22 days and the pool was already over two million dollars. Saturday didn't find a winner and Sunday came with some $2.4 million already in the pool. This is the last big day of the Santa Anita meet and a huge crowd is expected. There is no off-track betting in California and the record pool has attracted attention nationwide. Horse players from all over the US fly in that morning and large betting syndicates are formed to cover multiple-choice bets. I decline an invitation to join a $1000-a-head syndicate, using permutations of the fancied horses in all nine races, and set off for Santa Anita with Anthony and his daughter.

Santa Anita in Pasadena is the premier track in California, and provided there is enough of a breeze to keep the air clear of the LA smog the Santa Monica mountains provide a magnificent backdrop to the palm trees that fringe the track. Easter Sunday is a typically glorious Southern California day: blue skies with not a hint of cloud and a light wind. As we enter the racecourse we are caught up in the buzz of excitement which accompanies a big day's racing.

I have been studying the *Daily Racing Form*, a newspaper that gives all relevant information about the racing plus the experts' opinions and betting guides. Obviously, like everyone else attending the races that day, I am going to have a go at winning the Pick Nine. Today, however, there is a difference. Santa Anita has announced that if no one is able to find all nine winners, 70 percent of the pool will be paid out to the tickets with the greatest number of winners, while the remaining 30 percent will be divided between those having one or two fewer winners.

My selections have avoided the favourites as I never bet on short-priced horses and anyway I am sure the big syndicates will have covered all the permutations of favourites. I note that in two races trainer Mayberry and jockey McHargue are combining – knowing that this combination has been amongst the winners in the previous week, I select both horses. In the last race I see that there is a Frankel-trained horse ridden by Bill Shoemaker, one of the most senior jockeys riding who has brought home more than nine thousand winners. Bill is some-one I know well and one thing I do know is that Sunday evening is the night he likes to go out and party as there is no racing on a Monday. There is nothing he likes more on a Sunday evening than to perch on a bar stool at Chasen's in Beverly Hills and drink the night away with his pals. It's a cert that he wouldn't take a ride in the last race unless he felt it had a real chance. The horse is called Millbow and he is the last of my selections.

In the third race is a horse with the unlikely name of Chicken Dinner – I cannot conceive of a much worse name for a thoroughbred, but my fiancée Julie with whom I am living had asked to see the list of runners as she likes to pick horses by their names. Saturday night's supper was in the oven at the time and so Chicken Dinner appears in my list of selections, despite the fact it has never even been placed in a race, let alone won. This is the outsider of a seven-horse field at 20–1.

Having been shown to our lunch table in the Turf Club Anthony and I start filling in our Pick Nine tickets. By sheer coincidence we both invest $64, giving each of us five races with two selections and four races with one. In the first race I have picked the first Mayberry-trained runner Jan's Swifty, whose odds are 5–1. I have also put a separate bet on her and she wins quite easily, so I return to the table knowing that my losses if any for the day will be minimal. Anthony has also selected the first winner and the second race ends in a photo-finish between my selection Shrewd Steve, a 6–1 chance, and Anthony's choice Grand Vizier, a 12–1 shot. As our table is some 100 yards beyond the winning post we have no idea of which horse has won and we agree to pool our tickets in the unlikely event of either of us winning anything in the Pick Nine. In the event it is Shrewd Steve who wins by a nose and once more I pay a visit to the payout window. As I am well ahead I put a bet on Chicken Dinner, despite misgivings about the horse's ability, and am astounded when she romps home by six lengths at odds of 20–1. Laffit Pincay does the business for me in the fourth race on a horse called At The Ritz at 5–1 and I am beginning to believe I can walk on water.

In the fifth race I have two horses running for me, one a 4–1 shot and the other, Pokare, a rank outsider. This is a 6½-furlong sprint on the turf and Pokare is in the lead coming into the straight. I am starting to yell him home but inexplicably 100 yards from the finishing line he swerves away from the rail, allowing another horse to creep up on the inside and beat him by a head. My world comes crashing down as I have begun to have dreams of holding a winning Pick Nine ticket, but I am so far ahead on the day that I forget the disappointment very quickly. The sixth race provides me with another Mayberry–McHargue winner, this time at 8–1, and the man at the payout window is starting to make jokes with me as he hands over yet another sheaf of dollars.

The seventh race brings me back to earth with a bump as my selection is unplaced but I get the winner of the San Juan Capistrano so that my ticket has six out of eight possible winners so far. I realise the likelihood is that a big syndicate investing $100,000 or more will probably be able to cover enough combinations to get all nine winners, but no favourites have won so far, and if I were to get the last winner there's a possibility that if no ticket had all nine winners I would be eligible for a minor dividend.

We go down to the paddock for the final race and watch Shoemaker mount up on Millbow, then make a final visit to the betting window and back to watch the race. It is a mile race on the turf and Shoe's horse is 8–1 in a field of nine. He doesn't break well and sits in behind a wall of horses, on the far side he is lying fifth and I can see he is going well but there is no opening in front of him. The field enters the straight and Shoe is still behind the wall of horses looking for an opening on the rails, it doesn't come and Shoe tugs Millbow back and makes for the outside, a manoeuvre which will cost him valuable lengths. Finally there is a clear space in front of him, but only 75 yards to go as he urges Millbow forward. We are yelling 'Shoe, Shoe' for all we are worth and he thrusts the horse's head in front in the final strides.

Seven winners from nine races. Will it be enough to get a share of 15 percent of part of the pool. If no one has all nine winners we might be in line for $10,000 or more. There is a seemingly endless wait while the dividends for the race are declared. Trevor Denman, the track announcer, begins to list the exotic wager payouts. Exactas, trifectas, Pick Six. When will it end? Then in measured tones, he slowly announces, 'The Pick Nine pool amounted to four million dollars. There were – NO tickets with nine winners.' We look at each other in the realisation that my ticket is a winner of some sort. As Denman continues, 'There were NO tickets with eight winners', Anthony and I stare at each other with stunned silence, realising we have a share of 70 percent of the pool. How many other winning tickets will there be? Finally the announcement, 'There are – three tickets with seven winners, each paying $917,645.'

At this point, we cannot contain ourselves, leaping in the air and yelling like schoolboys. We make our way to the payout window and tell the cashier that we have a winning Pick Nine ticket. He inserts it into the machine, which instructs us to go to the tax window. The tax window is located one floor below and we proceed there, accompanied by a small crowd eager to witness our windfall. There's a queue at the tax window, and while we are waiting, someone shouts, 'These guys have got one of the winning Pick Nine tickets!' A man in front of us wearing a smart black and white hound's-tooth jacket asks if he can look at our ticket. I hand it over and he studies intensely. Suddenly he looks up at me and says, 'You've got two winning lines.'

I don't really understand what he means, but he goes into an explanation of how we had the first four winners and two losers in the fifth race, which means we had two lines carrying forward. This is a major surprise, which neither of us can quite take in. Then he says, 'You've got the consolation dividends for six winners and five winners as well.' Then he announces to the world in general, 'These guys are looking at a $2,000,000 ticket and they don't even know it!'

At this point, a Santa Anita official arrives and tells us to accompany him to the main Tote offices at the bottom of the building. The offices are jammed with people and we are told to take a seat and fill in tax forms, a necessity, as gambling winnings in the US are liable to tax. I tell the official we have been informed that our ticket may contain two winning lines. He smiles and tells us that the machine will give us the exact amount of our winnings. After some 15 minutes, the room is almost empty and we walk over to the counter, where the ticket is fed into the pari-mutuel machine. The total flashes up instantly in red numbers: $2,033,852.40. We have won over two million dollars for an outlay of $64, but 20 percent is going to have to go to Uncle Sam. We hand over our tax forms, duly completed, and are each given a cheque for $813,542.20. We could take cash, but having seen a good portion of the 50,000-plus crowd we reckon our chances of making it out of the car park intact are somewhat slim.

By now it is quite late and we both have dinner engagements. I drop Anthony and his daughter at his hotel and ask him to ring Julie to say I'll be back a bit late. Anthony rings Julie whose first question is, 'Did Chicken Dinner win?' Anthony tells her it did and she then asks if I won on the day; his reply is, 'I think Nick finished in front.' I arrive home a short time later and Julie asks how much I won. I say nothing but produce the cheque. I am still in a numb state of shock, and when I go to bed that night, I put the cheque on my bedside table. I wake up in the night and have to turn on the light in order to make sure it has not all been a dream.

The following day I take the cheque into my bank in Beverly Hills and my account manager is so impressed he insists on taking me round the bank to introduce me to all the vice-presidents. That night Anthony and I had been invited to dinner at Zoffany's trainer, John Gosden's house. Zoffany's jockey, Eddie Delahoussaye and his wife are there plus various inhabitants of the racing scene. There has been much talk about the Pick Nine, and the *Los Angeles Times* had a small line saying that two anonymous Englishmen had scooped two-thirds of the pool. Gosden is always an excellent host, loves to party and is never short of wine for his guests, and while we tell the assembled company the story of Easter Sunday, more and more bottles of wine are opened until we sit down to dinner in a haze of alcohol. Immediately dinner is over, we watch the videos of Zoffany's races with Eddie D until Gosden announces that for the first time in his life, he has run out of wine. The search of the kitchen cupboards reveals a bottle of cooking sherry and that is downed before we weave our way home.

Back in England there has been a mixed reaction to our win. The story appeared in Nigel Dempster's column in the *Daily Mail* some weeks later with the heading 'Nick's $1.6 million is just the ticket', describing it as 'the greatest racing jackpot in the history of the turf'. One remark from a fellow racing fan was reported to me verbatim. 'Have you seen this morning's mail? I nearly threw up into my cornflakes when I read about those lucky bastards in California.' On the other hand some inveterate gamblers wanted to hear the story in detail to get vicarious pleasure from reliving the event. Dan Meinertzhagen, a friend of both of ours, met Anthony at Aspinall's Club, shortly after the story broke, and insisted on hearing the day's event from the moment we woke up until we got back after the races. He, unlike some, was not in the remotest bit jealous, but explained that all his life he had dreamed of winning the 'Big One' and was delighted that friends of his had achieved it.

One less favourable reaction came from Julie's grandfather Jule Styne. Jule was the Broadway composer who wrote *Funny Girl* and *Gypsy* among other musicals and penned such standards as 'Diamonds are a Girl's Best Friend' and 'Three Coins in a Fountain'. Jule had been an addicted horse-player all his life and liked nothing better than to frequent the seediest betting parlours in New York, mixing with the hardest gamblers and perpetual losers that gather in these places. I had attended race meetings with him at Belmont and Aqueduct and had seen him bet on at least six horses in one race on occasions. This happened from listening to tips from everyone he knew at the track, and he knew plenty of people – waiters, trainers, barmen, Tote operators, owners or just other horse players. His style of betting meant he would often find a winner but almost invariably end the day out of pocket.

During the week after the Pick Nine I rang Jule to give him the good news, but before I could tell him anything, he asked me if I knew who the two anonymous Englishmen were. When I told him it was my ticket, I think he dropped the phone. There was silence for a few moments, and then he hung up. It was two years before he could bring himself to speak to me again.

The days after the win went by in a haze of celebratory dinners. Two week later I found myself in the Candlelight Wedding Chapel in Las Vegas tying the knot with Julie at half past midnight. The wording on the wedding certificate began: 'On this day in the City of Las Vegas, Clark County, Nevada, the lucky couple became big winners in the game of life when the pair recited their marriage vows. The groom laid his chips on the line to bet on his future and it paid off when the bride took a chance and sighed "I will." ' And so on with more in the same vein.

One postscript to the story is that Anthony, who stayed in LA for the following week, had an idea that a UK citizen might not be liable to US tax on gambling winnings. He consulted an attorney in LA who was well versed in all matters concerned with horse-racing. After recounting the story of our win,

Anthony was informed that as it was such a complex matter, the attorney would be unable to make a judgement until he had studied the case in greater detail. Three days later the attorney contacted Anthony to reiterate that this was an extremely complex case where he thought that Anthony might have a reasonable chance of recovering the tax paid, but in view of the work involved he would only undertake to represent Anthony on a one-third contingency basis, if successful in the claim. At the same time, he submitted a bill for $1200 for the four hours work he had already put in. Not being satisfied with this advice, Anthony returned to London and consulted his own lawyer. A US tax form was produced which Anthony filled in listing his US income, amounting solely to his gambling winnings. This was sent off in January 1988 and in May of that year he was assigned a temporary tax number from Philadelphia. Nothing more was heard until June, when an envelope arrived at his address from the US embassy in Grosvenor Square. It contained nothing other than a cheque for $203,834 from the US Treasury.

I knew nothing of this until later in the week, when Julie and I were invited to dinner at Anthony's house. When we sat down at the dinner table, I noticed an envelope propped up in front of my place with Zoffany written on it. Intrigued, I opened it, suddenly aware that all eyes were on me. Inside was the cheque with a note saying, 'American lawyers are shysters.' It transpired that Anthony had had a bill for £73.50 from his lawyer for his services. Subsequently Anthony wrote to the attorney he had consulted in LA enclosing copies of the cheque and his lawyer's bill, pointing out that he had saved himself some $67,000 by not taking his advice. To the great credit of the attorney, he replied congratulating Anthony on his 'perspicacity' and refunding $600 of his own bill! This tax refund increased our overall winnings to over $2,000,000 and earned us a place in the

Guinness Book of World Records, where it remained for twelve years.

Chicken Dinner continued running on the Californian race-tracks for several years but never won another race.

16

At the Races

When I was seven years old my father took me to the races at Leopardstown in County Dublin. I was given two shillings to bet on a horse of my choice. I plumped for a horse with a 'Nick' in its name, Nicorino, which came in at odds of 20–1. From that day on I have had an abiding interest in horse-racing both as a gambler and in later years as an owner. By the time I was eighteen I was reading the *Sporting Life* on a daily basis and every Saturday found me at one race track or another.

Much of the appeal of horse-racing is the people involved in this Sport of Kings. Owners, trainers, bloodstock agents, punters and jockeys are amongst my friends, all of us engaged in an endless conflict against the bookmakers. We swap tips, debate form and may win a battle or two, but ultimately we know the bookies will win the war. There are many characters from all walks of life who contribute to the atmosphere of a day at the races. This chapter profiles a few of them.

In my younger days the most visible and vociferous person on the racetrack was the self-styled Prince Monolulu, who dressed as a Zulu chieftain. His war cry was 'I gotta 'orse.' His tips were no better or no worse than the next man's but his tribal warrior's outfit and strident voice made him the king of tipsters. One day on the race train to Brighton he talked me into a game of poker. I arrived at the races penniless and resolved never again to plays cards on a race train.

Of all the characters I came across in the world of horse-racing in the US, none was more ebullient, outgoing and opinionated than the bloodstock agent Billy MacDonald. An Irishman through and through with an answer to everything, Billy was as round as he was tall. If he'd had a family motto it would have been 'everything to excess'. The licence plate on his Maserati in California was ALLEGED, the name of the horse he bought for Robert Sangster which was champion horse in Europe in 1977 and won Europe's most prestigious race, the Prix de l'Arc de Triomphe, two years in succession. There was no one he didn't know in the racing world. In spite of this and all the tips he was given by jockeys, trainers and owners, he was not known for his success as a punter and was often short of funds. Whenever he had a sizeable win he was as generous as can be and the winnings would be dissipated in record time in fine wine, expensive restaurants and pretty girls.

Many were the times I went to the races in California with Billy and if the day was very successful we might move on to Las Vegas for 24 hours, usually to pass on the winnings from the horses to the card tables in the casino. One day in particular was remarkable for the size of the win; we had correctly forecast the first three home in a race, a rare winning trifecta which paid very long odds. We spent some time after the last race in the ornate bar of the club house at Santa Anita where a group of regulars gathered. Billy was buying drinks for everyone and decided we would go straight from the track to Burbank airport to fly to Las Vegas. He telephoned one of his connections there to make sure we were 'comped' with a suite at the Desert Inn.

Collecting a couple of friends to make up a foursome, we set off for the airport with Billy at the wheel. It must be said that Billy, after dealing with numerous cocktails in quick succession, was driving somewhat erratically. We were cruising down the freeway a few miles from the track when the red light of a California Highway Patrol car appeared in the rear-view mirror. Billy pulled over to the side of the road, complaining as one of the officers approached that he had been driving well within the speed limit. The officer circled our car briefly and, apparently satisfied that we were not hoodlums, came up to the driver's window which Billy had lowered.

'What seems to be the problem?' said Billy.

'You were all over the road going from one lane to another,' replied the officer, his face now close to Billy's as he peered into the car. By then he must have caught a whiff of Billy's brandy-laden breath. 'And I have reason to believe you're driving under the influence of alcohol.'

Before anyone in the car could stop him, Billy pointed his index finger at the officer, uttering the words, 'I'm going to nominate you for Detective of the Year.'

Within moments we were all out of the car, hands behind our heads, bent over the bonnet as the officer and his partner frisked us for weapons or drugs (of which we had neither). Efficient the California Highway Patrol may be, but its officers are not known for their sense of humour. It seemed that the trip to Vegas was out of the question as the Detective of the Year was intent on taking Billy into custody. One of Billy's many attributes, however, is that he never stops talking, and having learned that the officer's partner name was O'Regan he had engaged him in a conversation about Ireland. By a remarkable coincidence it transpired that Billy had been born in the same village as the officer's father. Not only did this get Billy off the hook but the officer took over the wheel and drove us to Burbank airport while his partner cleared the way ahead in the patrol car.

With a lucky break like that we knew we must be going to win when we got to Las Vegas. But things didn't turn out as expected. By the early hours of the next morning only Billy and I were left at the tables. A hour later and we too were cleaned out. Billy decided he needed some female company. Six a.m. on a Sunday morning is the graveyard shift when only the most hardened punters are at the few tables which remain open, while the cleaners circle with vacuums. Billy spots a lady of the night sitting at the bar. It is not a pretty sight. She must be a pensioner, but then no one else is going to be waiting around at this hour. Billy, who has been partaking of the free drinks all night, is not deterred. In his charming Irish brogue he invites the harridan up to the suite for some champagne and disappears into one of the bedrooms with her. I turn on the TV for the early morning news.

Some twenty minutes later there is a tremendous commotion within the bedroom. The door opens and the female is pushed into the suite, all the time cursing and threatening to call security. Billy appears in the doorway, beaming from ear to ear. He has turned his trouser pockets inside out and is holding them out like the ears of an elephant. As soon as he can get a word in he addresses the female: 'Surely by now you know the first rule of your profession,' he says. 'Always, always get the money up front.'

The woman knows she is defeated and leaves, cursing Billy as she goes.

It was Billy who introduced me to Laffit Pincay, one of the greatest jockeys of all time. When he retired in 2003 he had ridden 9,530 winners. Laffit was tall for a jockey and had a battle with his weight for the whole of his professional life. He needed to exercise an iron determination in order to keep down to his riding weight. That degree of determination was demonstrated when one day I was invited to his birthday party. Laffit lived in a house in Pasadena near Santa Anita racetrack. The party was on a Sunday after racing. Laffit's wife had prepared a lavish spread for about fifty people. There were sides of smoked salmon to be eaten American-style with cream cheese and bagels, together with plates of cold ham, roast beef and turkey, with half a dozen different breads. Cakes, cookies, chocolates and other calorific desserts were in abundance. The guests were mainly racing people, owners, trainers and a few other jocks. I was curious about Laffit's diet and wondered what he would do in the face of so many goodies.

Some bowls of peanuts had been passed around with the champagne before the meal. I watched as Laffit studied a bowl of nuts and carefully selected one single kernel. He put it on a plate and sat down with some other guests. Taking a knife he meticulously cut the peanut into four equal quarters which he arranged in a square on his plate. Taking plenty of time he picked up a quarter and put it in his mouth. He chewed slowly as if it were the finest kobe beef. After a ten-minute pause he dealt with another quarter in the same way. In half an hour he had finished his meal, consisting of exactly one peanut washed down with a cup of lemon tea. He explained that he was riding in a valuable handicap the next day and couldn't take the risk of being a pound overweight even though it was his birthday.

Another jockey who was at that party, Bill Shoemaker, had no such problem. Bill was only 4 feet 11 inches tall and could eat and drink whatever he wanted without putting on weight. Pound for pound, he was the greatest jockey that ever rode a racehorse as well as being a true gentleman. I knew Bill 'the Shoe' quite well and he and his wife Cindy had often been guests at my house. Shoe had a thing for tall girls. Cindy was his third wife and at 6 feet 1 inch was the tallest of the lot. Billy used to say of Cindy and Shoe,

> When they are nose to nose his toes are in it,
> When they are toes to toes his nose is in it.

Shoe retired from riding in 1990 and took up training. It was around this time that I was enjoying another stroke of luck on the racecourse. A couple of years earlier my trainer in England, Charlie James, had bought a filly for me in Ireland for around £7,000, a very modest price for a thoroughbred. She was by Alzao out a mare called Kaniz, so I named her Alcando. She won four races as a two-year-old and moved up in class to win a Group 3 race at Deauville the following year. As I was living in California I decided to ship her to the US and sent her to be trained by Bill Shoemaker. Although she flopped in her first race in the US, the prestigious Beverly D at Arlington Park in Chicago, she flourished in California. She won her prep race at Golden Gate Fields and was entered in the Beverly Hills Handicap, a Group 1 and one of the most valuable races of the year to be run at Hollywood Park.

Before that race came around Shoe suffered a terrible car accident which left him paralysed from the neck down. He was in a rehabilitation centre in Denver when the Beverly Hills handicap was run in June 1991. Alcando was the outsider of the field at 30–1 and confounded the experts by leading from start to finish. All owners dream of winning a Group 1 race. Fortunes are paid for thoroughbreds which never achieve this pinnacle of racing. To do so with a horse costing a mere £7,000 is something of a miracle. I was happy to have provided the Shoe with his first Group 1 winner. The following year Alcando went back to Arlington for another crack at the Beverly D. This time she won her prep race at Arlington, a Breeders Cup Handicap, beating the best filly in Canada who was the hot favourite. She ran poorly in the Beverly D, finishing nearer last than first. After the race I met the legendary trainer Charlie Whittingham in the unsaddling enclosure. Charlie, who also had a runner in the Beverly D, had been the leading trainer in California for many years and was then in his seventies. He was a man of very few words and he summed up Alcando's performance very succinctly, 'Hello Nick,' he said,

'Your filly ran shit.' Alcando was retired to stud in Kentucky where she produced a number of winning offspring.

The Bald Eagle, as Charlie was known thanks to his bald pate and hawkish nose, had a dry sense of humour. His fellow-trainer John Gosden was Charlie's main rival in turf races. When John told him he was leaving California to train in England for an Arab sheik, Charlie raised his eyebrows. 'Help you pack?' he suggested with a mischievous smile. I went to Charlie's 75th birthday celebration where a large number of racing people gathered to honour him. After we had drunk a toast to his health he was called upon to speak. True to form, the Bald Eagle got to his feet holding several sheets of paper and put his glasses on as if to begin the oration. He looked around the room for a moment, took off his glasses and with a 'Thanks for coming' sat down to enjoy his cake.

Anyone who aspires to become a racehorse trainer has probably been involved in the racing business all his life. At the very least he would feel it absolutely necessary to spend a few years as an assistant to an established trainer to learn the ropes. Not so Denny Cordell, whose technique was simply to buy every published book on the subject, immerse himself in the theory of training and breeding thoroughbreds, the launch himself as a public trainer of horses in Ireland. He applied the same dedicated research to the breeding of greyhounds. At one time, in his quest to breed a strain that would run faster than all other dogs, he owned several hundred of the animals.

Although DC had a modicum of success, his theory was not born out in practice. His knowledge of the bloodlines of racehorses was undeniably immense, but apart from a couple of exceptions the horses he bred did not amount to very much. He was certainly not in the same class as the late Robert Sangster, who was one of the most successful owners and breeders the sport has known. I was fortunate enough to count him as a good and generous friend, having joined him in a syndicate a few years ago which purchased several expensive animals. But in horse-racing things rarely go to plan. Horses win when they are least expected to and more often than not disappoint when a win seems on the cards. As punters, or owners, we tend to forget the bad days and the trainer's excuses and remember only the best of times. One of our worst days, however, has not faded from my memory.

The best of the animals in our syndicate was royally bred and ran well as a two-year-old. At three she was entered in one of the first prestigious races for her age and on the day of the race was the favourite in the betting. I had a commitment in Ireland and could not be at Newbury to watch the race. I settled down with Ronnie Wood at his house in County Kildare to watch the race on TV. We had made friends with a professional punter who bet thousands of pounds every day and claimed to have information from every well-known trainer's stable. Half an hour before the race was due to go off our friend called to say that he had heard from his mole in the trainer's yard that our horse was not right and would not win. I managed to telephone Robert at Newbury racecourse where he was lunching with our trainer and the other syndicate members. Robert conferred with the trainer, who confirmed all was well and in any event said he had already made a large bet. The horse ran deplorably and finished last, beaten twenty lengths. We never knew what was wrong with the horse on that day and he continued to disappoint until we gave up and sold out at a loss.

A better day was had when Ronnie Wood and I went to the Curragh racetrack for the Irish Derby in 1990 with Denny, who was then enjoying a winning streak as a trainer. The race before the Derby is always a competitive handicap with a large number of runners. Denny had trained a horse for this race and I was delegated to place a bet for all of us. The bookmakers' odds were 33–1 but I saw that the odds on the Tote were much longer. I fought my way through the crowds to the Tote window and put all our ready cash on the nose to win. The horse duly obliged and the Tote odds were 85–1. I needed a wheelbarrow to collect the winnings. The next day the *Irish Times* reported as follows: 'Rolling Stone Ronnie Wood was seen at the Curragh divvying up fistfuls of readies with his manager and Denny Cordell, the winning trainer of the Scurry Handicap.' Days like that are rare indeed.

Rod Stewart

I first met Rod when I lived in New York in the mid-1980s and was asked to host a party for the artists who performed in a fundraiser for ARMS, the fund set up to help those suffering from multiple sclerosis. Rod and Ronnie Wood were performing along with their old band mate from The Faces Ronnie Lane, who had contracted MS some years earlier and was on stage in a wheelchair.

At the height of their fame in the '70s The Faces were known as much for their antics off-stage as their live shows performed with a bar on stage. They originated the TV-out-of-the-hotel-window game which became legendary. Another favourite on tour was to remove every single item of furniture from the hotel suite and reassemble it in another public area of the hotel, then call the manager and complain about the draught.

After Rod left to pursue a solo career and Ronnie became a full-time member of the Stones they remained pals but saw little of each other. Although not averse to a few drinks and the occasional line, Rod disapproved of what he considered to be Ronnie's excessive lifestyle.

The ARMS concert in New York was one of the few times I saw them together in the '80s. The minute Rod and Ronnie saw each other it was like the old days with The Faces. They lapsed into a dialogue using a private language of their own. No outsider could understand their conversation, which involved extreme facial contortions coupled with in-jokes between themselves and invented words. They had developed this language to such a degree that Rod wrote a number of nonsense poems, including one called 'My Dad's Trousers', which I tried to get published as a book with illustrations by Ronnie. Sadly, no publisher would touch it despite the fame of the authors, probably because they were the only two people in the world who could understand the verses.

The party in my house began not long after the concert finished. Guests and friends of guests appeared and began downing alcohol at an impressive rate. From then on it was like watching an episode of 'Survival of the Fittest'. After a couple of hours Rod had had enough and left, followed at intervals by various friends and freeloaders who staggered out into the night. By early morning the only people left standing were Ronnie and two Texan friends of Ronnie Lane's who had flown in specially for the event. In these conditions Ronnie was completely bombproof and happy to continue drinking and talking till nobody was left. Finally the two Texans lurched off mumbling about T-bone steaks and eggs for breakfast, leaving me to contemplate the debris littered around the house. As I was about to go to bed for a couple of hours sleep I noticed a woman's shoe sticking out from behind a sofa – it turned out to be attached to the foot of Marianne Faithfull who was fast asleep on the floor.

It was not until I had moved to Beverly Hills that I really got to know Rod, who by then was married to Rachel Hunter. I never represented Rod in any professional way but spent a lot of time in his company during his years with Rachel. We were near neighbours in Beverly Hills and my then wife Julie was a close friend of Rachel's. We enjoyed many a Sunday lunch at each other's homes, dinners at Le Dome, Rod's favourite restaurant in Los Angeles, visits to Santa Anita race-track and some trips abroad. Rod's obsession with football, sex and money coupled with a laddish sense of humour ensured he was a man's man, which perhaps explains why he failed to settle down for the long term and instead enjoyed a succession of relationships, including marriages to a series of beautiful women.

At this time Ronnie Wood had released a solo album, *Slide on This*. He produced this in his studio in Ireland and then came over to the US to do some shows in several cities to promote it. He was staying with me in my house in Coldwater Canyon for his LA show and of course Rod was to be one of the guests of honour. At one point during the show Ronnie started to play 'Ooh-La-La', one of The Faces' biggest hits, hoping to induce Rod to join him on the stage, but despite my urgings and Ronnie's entreaties Rod wouldn't budge. He had reached the stage where unless there was some financial gain to be made he wasn't interested in impromptu performances. He was, however, so impressed with Ronnie's dexterity on guitar that he invited him to join him as a special guest on his MTV 'Unplugged and Seated' album.

During Ronnie's stay in LA Rod and Rachel came to dinner at our house, which was not far from Rod's home in Beverly Park. After many drinks and much merriment we struck up a friendship which lasted until my parting of the ways with Ronnie. During the course of that evening Rod and I managed to break the telephone as we both reached for it at the same time. From then on he liked to call me 'one-line management'.

Not long after our meeting I had my first experience of a dinner party at Rod's house. Within the exclusive enclave of Beverly Park, a gated and guarded development of multi-million dollar homes, Rod and Rachel had built a magnificent home that was part French chateau and part Scottish baronial. Antiques, collectables, memorabilia and works of art were on display everywhere. With a keen eye for a bargain, Rod had been collecting Victorian art, including several paintings by Burne-Jones, long before prices for that artist went sky-high. The palatial house in Beverly Hills is just one of Rod's homes. He has another equally sumptuous mansion in Palm Beach, Florida, and a country house near Epping in England complete with its own football pitch, called 'Wood House'.

After a glass or two of champagne the dinner guests were seated in the baronial dining hall. Rod favours the Aussie seating plan – girls at one end of the table and blokes at the other. The guests were a mixed group of ex-pats including several members of Rod's very own football team, some fellow musicians, a music business manager and a Scot with an accent so thick I found it impossible to discover what he was doing in Los Angeles. Wives and girlfriends made up the numbers.

The food was elaborate and a chef was employed for the night. The wine, it must be admitted, although plentiful was of dubious quality. At a given signal the lights dimmed and there was much shifting in their seats by the men. Moments later Rod and the male guests rose to their feet, glasses in hand and trousers around their ankles. One of the guests who missed the pre-dinner briefing for Rod's favourite prank had shyly omitted to drop his trousers. 'Show us your block and tackle,' yelled Rod, grinning from ear to ear. Although this side-splitting jape was being repeated for the umpteenth time, Rod and his mates were in fits of laughter. Diners at top restaurants around the world have witnessed this same scene. It is not unknown for Rod and his mates to keep their trousers down for the entire length of a meal.

Traditional English Sunday lunch was a must whenever Rod was in town. He likes his meat well-done with plenty of vegetables, always including cauliflower cheese. We used to take it in turns to have Sunday lunch at each other's houses.

When dining out Rod acts the gentleman. Bobbing up and down in his seat like a yo-yo every time a female comes and goes to the lavatory, he is the epitome of old-fashioned behaviour and manners, now rarely seen in his contemporaries – until, that is, the bill arrives. Then there is much fumbling in the pockets for the forgotten credit card which has been left at home again. A low-denomination banknote might sometimes be produced as a modest contribution, but it is only when his record label is picking up the expenses that Rod pays the bill. 'Tight as two coats of paint' is one of Ronnie Wood's phrases for him. Another colleague of Rod's described him as 'so tight you couldn't swipe a credit card between the cheeks of his arse'.

Curiously, Rod actually delights in maintaining his reputation as a skinflint. At a filming of a TV special at Thames studios in London before an invited audience of selected celebrities, members of the audience were invited to ask questions. After fielding a couple of standard questions about the blondes in his life Rod saw British comedian Vic Reeves get to his feet.

'What would you do if a penny rolled under the fridge in your kitchen? Would you try and retrieve it?' Vic asked mischievously.

'I certainly would,' said Rod. 'Even if I had to pull the fridge out to get it!'

Much has been made in the media of Rod's legendary meanness, but it has to be said that when it comes to larger expenses Rod can be as generous as the next man. For many years he and Ronnie Wood paid Ronnie Lane's bills and medical expenses through my office.

Rod is keen on horse-racing and we often went to the Californian tracks together. He likes a bet and if he fancies a horse strongly is happy to put on a few hundred dollars.

Unlike some of the other gamblers around him he doesn't curse the jockey, the horse or the trainer if he loses. In July the racing in California moves out of LA to Del Mar near San Diego and occasionally Rod would hire a private jet to ferry himself and some friends to the races for the day. On one such jaunt, halfway though the afternoon I was telephoned with the news that my wife was on her way to hospital and about to give birth to a baby which was one month premature. As Del Mar is close to San Diego and several hours drive to Los Angeles it would have been impossible for me to get to the hospital in time by road.

'Don't worry,' said Rod. 'I can get you a helicopter to the hospital.' He called his charter company, all was arranged, and within an hour I was landing on the roof of Cedars Sinai hospital a hundred miles away. I missed the birth of my son by twenty minutes and received a hefty bill for the helicopter a week later. Rod's generosity goes only so far.

There is instant recognition for Rod wherever he goes. He complains all the time about not being able to go out without being accosted by the general public, but at the same time he never ceases to draw attention to himself. With the dress sense of an eighteenth-century dandy he favours bright colours, loud checks, contrasting waistcoats and designer labels. And with his gel-spiked straw hair he is never going to merge into the crowd. Of course the reality is that he craves attention and abhors the thought of being anonymous.

Sex, money and football (in any order) are Rod's main topics of conversation. When these subjects are exhausted, he has little to say about anything else. Never one to hold back in discussion, he is prone to open the conversation with a question such as 'How much have you got in the Bank today?' or (over breakfast) 'Did you give her one last night?' If Rachel goes to bed early while Rod waits up for the football results, he will tell her to be good and ready for him later.

Rachel has her own response to that: 'Don't forget to pull my nightie down when you've finished.'

When holidays come round Rod will charter a gin-palace of a yacht and cruise the Mediterranean with his family and a few guests. In the summer of 1991 my family and I were Rod's guests aboard the yacht *Venezia* together with Rachel, her sister Jackie and several of Rod's children. We spent the time cruising between Cannes and St Tropez, usually going ashore for meals, where we could be sure to join some other folk who would be happy to pick up the bill for the privilege of sitting down to a meal with Rod.

Rod has a laddish sense of humour, provided the joke is on someone else. The *Venezia* was an old-fashioned yacht with a crew of six. On the main deck were some electric capstans operated by buttons set into the floor of the deck. These capstans had a particular fascination for my seven year-old son Christopher, who would watch intently when the crew stood on the buttons to wind in the ropes which would keep the yacht steady in port.

One day, while we were at anchor off the coast of Cannes, Christopher couldn't resist the temptation of standing on one of the buttons and watching the capstan turn. The rope coming off this particular capstan was tied to the tender, which the wind had moved around to the other side of the yacht. As the line went taut the tender was dragged against the side of the *Venezia* and began to be pulled down into the water as the rope tried to haul it under the yacht. The rope must have been close to breaking-point when a crew member took Christopher's foot off the button. The line was so taut the crew were unable to release the rope and the irate captain had no option but to bring up the anchor and manoeuvre the yacht around in order to release the tender. Christopher received a serious dressing-down from the captain, but Rod took it all in his stride and treated the incident as a joke.

In 1993 Rod made an album and TV special for MTV in the 'Unplugged and Seated' series. Ronnie Wood was his special guest. Some of Rod's best songs from the early days were co-written with Ronnie, including 'Gasoline Alley' and 'Every Picture Tells A Story'. It was during the negotiations for Ronnie's participation as a special guest that I first met Rod's manager Arnold Steiffel. When I first went to his office and he discovered that I was married to the granddaughter of Jule Styne, the Broadway composer, he was beside himself with excitement. Jule's musicals *Gypsy* and *Funny Girl* were Arnold's favourites and he was lost in admiration for the vast catalogue of standards that Jule had written. I suggested that Rod might one day do an album of Jule's songs and I like to think that was the seed for the hugely successful American songbook series that Rod recorded some years later.

My relationship with Arnold was not always cordial and when Rod made his recordings for MTV it went further down-hill. I had been expecting Arnold to contact me to agree a deal for Ronnie's participation, but the day of the recording came and went without a word from Arnold. This was a little strange but I put it down to the fact that Arnold was busy negotiating deals for Rod's future appearances at private parties and concerts. But several days after the recording was finished I had a call from Arnold in which he proposed that Ronnie should merely get three times the standard union-scale musician's fee. There was no mention of royalties at all.

This was the old-fashioned Hollywood agent's attempt to screw as much money as possible out of a deal, but I was having none of it. Arnold's position was weak, despite his bluster, because the recording was already in the can and he was in no position to negotiate. Quite clearly, Ronnie's name and the fact that he added so much to the recording would help it become a best-seller, as indeed it did. So I insisted on Ronnie receiving a share of the royalties, and Arnold with bad grace was forced to concede. He called me a few unflattering names and we were never on the best of terms afterwards. I suspect part of the trouble lay in the fact that Julie and I were on such friendly terms with the Stewarts, taking holidays together and dining out in LA, whereas Arnold was considered purely as a business manager and was rarely present on social occasions.

Some time later Arnold rang me to ask whether Ronnie could appear with Rod as a guest on some tour dates in Los Angeles and San Francisco. Ronnie was staying with me in LA at the time and I thought he would like to do the dates. However, I had to check with the Stones' office that there was no conflict as a tour was approaching. The response was that Ronnie's presence would be needed elsewhere by the Stones. In the meantime Arnold had jumped the gun before we had reached a formal agreement and I heard some ads on the car radio announcing that Ronnie would be appearing as a guest at some of the concerts. When I called Arnold to tell him to pull the ads as Ronnie wouldn't be appearing, he completely lost his cool.

'You can take your burnt-out guitarist and stick him up your arse,' were his words to me.

For once in my life I was able to forestall *l'esprit d'escalier* with an immediate reply: 'You know a lot more about sticking things up arses than I do.' This was not lost on Arnold, a self-professed gay. When Rod and I were having a laugh about the exchange later on, Rod called Arnold to give him a telling-off. 'It was just good natured banter between managers,' Arnold told Rod.

There is no doubt that Rod was infatuated with Rachel. Being a tall, well-built girl she towered over him, and it was clear she was one who wore the trousers. She would choose the restaurant for dinner, decide the menu, organise the holidays and generally give the orders. Rod was possessive to a high degree and it was trouble for anyone who looked at Rachel too intently. In 1998 Sheikh Mohammed of Dubai was seeking global recognition for the Dubai World Cup, the world's richest horse race. As a friend of John Leat, the Sheikh's right hand man, I was asked if I could arrange for some celebrities to come to Dubai for the racing in order to attract publicity to the event. Rod and Rachel were ideal candidates to get the attention of the newsreel cameras and the world's press and it took little persuasion to get them to go. We were flown to Dubai, where we were accommodated in great luxury. On the evening before the big race we were with a group of friends from England in the hotel bar enjoying several after-dinner drinks. Rachel dropped a lipstick from her handbag and went down on her hands and knees to retrieve it. In so doing her head was at crotch level with one of the group, who had perhaps had several drinks too many and happened to be one of the many bloodstock agents employed by the ruling family of Dubai. He was foolish enough to crack a doubtful joke, saying to Rachel 'While you're down there do me a favour and give me a bl . . . '

He didn't get to finish the sentence as Rod pulled Rachel to her feet and stormed out of the bar, having suffered a complete sense of humour failure. The problem didn't end there. Rod announced the next morning that he and Rachel were returning to Los Angeles and would not stay for the race, which was the main reason for their invitation to Dubai. It was only after much pleading and the delivery of a grovelling apology that Rod relented and agreed to stay. Rachel had good reason to be pleased that they did. Whilst we were being given a guided tour of the Sheikh's polo grounds and stables she was particularly taken with an animal that she thought was the most beautiful pony she had ever seen. On hearing her appreciation of the polo pony our Arab hosts arranged for it be shipped to Rod's house in Essex as a gift.

Five years after Rod and Rachel were married, they decided to renew their marriage vows. The ceremony and party were organised at the Compleat Angler, an inn on the banks of the Thames, an hour from London. All of Rod's family and a small number of his friends were invited. Needless to say, the cost of the event was covered by an exclusive spread in *Hello!*, which was just as well since Rod and Rachel were wearing outfits designed and tailored for the occasion. The high point at dinner occurred when a silver dome-covered platter was put in front of Rod and upon the raising of the lid Rachel's hairpiece was revealed.

Van Morrison had penned one of Rod's biggest hits, 'Have I Told You Lately That I Love You?', which Rod sang as an ode to Rachel. A dinner was arranged in London after the song had gone to number 1 in the pop charts. Rod invited Van Morrison, the Woods, myself and Julie and another couple to Langans restaurant. The reservation was made for 9 pm but although we were all there on time there was no sign of Van Morrison. Nine o'clock came and went and we all ordered dinner. We were finishing our main course some 45 minutes later when we became aware of a commotion at the door of the restaurant. In staggered Van Morrison, wearing a hat and sunglasses and shaking off the attentions of an anxious doorman. Conversation in the restaurant had by now almost stopped and everybody watched in fascination to see the next development. After stumbling into a couple into a couple of tables Van Morrison spotted our group and slumped into the empty chair. Food did not seem to be uppermost in his mind as he was content to grab a glass of wine, turn away from us and harangue every passing female, saying he wanted to get laid. Unsurprisingly this tactic met with little success, but when he turned his attentions to the girls at our table, Rod decided he had had enough and we left Van Morrison sitting there in a drunken stupor.

New Year's Eve 1998 was spent with Rod and Rachel at the Ritz Hotel in London. Rod had chosen the Ritz because the New Year is ushered in with a piper in full highland dress marching round the restaurant playing 'Auld Lang Syne' on the bagpipes at full volume. Earlier in the day Ronnie had sent me a fax saying he could not make it over from Ireland as they were snowed in. He sent a drawing of his house in Ireland with the faces of himself and his wife pressed against the window with the snow piling up. Rod was unimpressed and decided Ronnie had been partying too much over Christmas and didn't feel like making the trip to London for New Year's Eve, which had been planned weeks before. Actually it was the first time in many years that there had been a white Christmas in Ireland and when Ronnie said they couldn't make it down the drive of their house this was the simple truth.

I had also been with Rod and Ronnie Wood at Royal Ascot in that year. After the races we went to a party at John Leat's house in Sunningdale. Rod was persuaded to sing a few numbers with what was probably the strangest line-up he had ever performed with. The London jeweller Theo Fennell was playing the spoons and George Stevens, the American champion jockey who was riding at Ascot, was on drums. Amongst the crowd was Andrew Lloyd Webber whose Oscar statuette had been stolen a few days earlier. Rod sang a little ditty he made up on the spot, 'Andrew, Where's Your Oscar?', perhaps because Andrew had declined the request to play piano. Rod loved the party as there were footballers and ex-footballers present, among them Gary Lineker and Brian Robson. Vinnie Jones, who was also there, lived up to expectations by flattening F1 boss Eddie Jordan with a right hook because he thought Eddie was making advances to his wife. All in all, a memorable evening.

A few years later, after he and Rachel had parted, Rod was dating Caprice, a model famed for her statuesque body. On the occasion of my wife's fortieth birthday party in Tramp, Rod got it into his head that champion jockey Frankie Dettori was hitting on Caprice, when in fact he was just being his usual cheeky and sociable self. Rod took umbrage and left the party, taking Caprice with him.

Over the years there have been a number of attempts to get the surviving members of The Faces back on tour. The public demand is there but Rod has never really wanted to do it. At one time he told me he was up to it and I began making enquiries of promoters. Some time later he later pulled out by having Arnold Steiffel tell me, with great satisfaction, that it was not going to happen. I suspect the reason is that Rod has no desire to split the profits with the other band members when he can go out on his own as a solo artist and keep the lot for himself.

After my split with Ronnie Wood in 2002 I did not see Rod again.

18

Benny Hill

For many years the Benny Hill Show was one of the most popular on British TV. It was also watched in more than 100 countries around the world. Nevertheless the time came in 1989 when Thames Television, which had been the home of the show for 14 years, decided to drop it. Times had changed and the era of political correctness was upon us. There were many who thought his particular brand of comedy was just harmless fun, but Benny was deemed to be racist, politically incorrect and, above all, much too sexist.

Benny was a true original. Unlike many comedians, he did not employ teams of gag writers, editors or executive producers. Every word of his shows was written by him. He also wrote all the music to his many comic songs, one of which, 'Ernie The Fastest Milkman In The West', went to the top of the UK hit parade. David Cameron included 'Ernie' in his selection for Desert Island Discs in 2006. In some countries, notably France, he is revered as a genius on a par with Chaplin.

Benny was devastated by Thames's decision to drop him, for which he was entirely unprepared. After all, they were making a fortune selling the shows to foreign countries. But having picked himself up, he began to have ideas for a new project. For this, though he was himself a very rich man who lived a very frugal life, he needed a business backer.

Benny had conceived the idea of making a spoof version of the MTV music awards, in which he would play not only all the judges but also all the characters competing for awards.

The idea was brought to me by Adrian Hilliard, a friend of Benny's long-time director Dennis Kirkland. As this was to be a one-off special for TV, they were finding it difficult to raise financing for the project from broadcasters, who will always prefer a series. I was a huge fan of Benny's comedy and believed that not only would it make for a TV special with global appeal, but it would also give us a complete album of Benny's songs to distribute.

A meeting was arranged with Benny for lunch in his home base of Twickenham where he rented a small flat. We met at his local pub for his favourite meal, fish and chips with mushy peas. Focusing on the business of the TV special was no easy matter since it was Benny's practice to deliver a constant stream of one-liners which had everyone laughing.

I had arrived alone and explained to Benny that my partner who had agreed to provide the funding had been taken ill. 'Sorry he couldn't make it. He wasn't feeling himself this morning,' I said in all innocence.

'Oh, why was that?' said Benny with a twinkle in his eye. 'Looking for his keys in his pocket, was he?'

As lunch progressed the question of financing the project was brought up by Dennis Kirkland, and Benny looked serious for a moment. 'No problem there,' he said, 'Nick is providing the money.' With this he pulled out a plastic water pistol and held it to my head.

'And now we're all going to have Southamptons to celebrate,' Benny continued.

'Oh? What are those?' I asked.

'Large ports, of course,' chuckled Benny. And so it went on.

After several toasts to the success of the project, the discussion turned to the subject of food. I asked Benny why the press portrayed him as a miser who would walk miles to buy a cut-price tin of beans. He explained that he was a compulsive eater and had a constant battle with his weight. If he bought six tins of beans at a time he would go home and eat all six, and so he only shopped in small quantities on a daily basis. He did not drive a car and rarely took taxis, preferring to walk in the belief that it would help him keep his weight down. He thought nothing of walking the twelve miles from home to visit his dentist in Harley Street.

Much of his life was spent in an armchair in front of the television as he dreamed up new ideas for his shows.

It was agreed that first we would record the album, at Abbey Road Studios, and later Adrian's company would shoot the video in Florida where Benny was due to appear as one of the judges of the Miss Hawaiian Tropic pageant. Benny was filmed crossing Abbey Road in the style of the famous Beatles album cover and made a pastiche appearance for the video as the doorman at Abbey Road. Nobody got past him without slipping a £20 note into his pocket. The twelve songs, all composed by Benny, were recorded with a full orchestra in three days.

As each of the songs featured a different style and setting we arranged to shoot the videos at Universal Studios in Florida, where sets have been built representing various locations from a New York street to a cowboy rodeo. Three videos were completed – one with Benny as leather-jacketed rapper in New York, another where he was a country-and-western cowboy singer, and the third a Hawaiian-themed song among the palm trees. We also shot some footage of Benny cavorting with the Hawaiian Tropic lovelies and joking around with Leslie Nielsen, star of the movies *Airplane* and *The Naked Gun*. Benny appeared in an ancient one-piece swimming costume looking hugely overweight.

Before we could return to Florida to shoot the remainder of the videos Benny was taken ill and hospitalised in February 1992. He never recovered and died at his flat in Twickenham the following April. The album of comic songs was released later that year but because we had only sixteen minutes of video film, it never made it onto the TV screens and the costs of making the video were never recouped.

The fate of Benny's estate may be taken as a warning to all those of us who fail to update our wills so as to reflect our most recent intentions. Benny had promised several close friends, including his director/producer Dennis Kirkland and several ex-girlfriends, that they would benefit from his estate. But he never changed the will that he had made quite early on in his life, leaving everything to his parents. They were now long dead and so all of his multi-million pound estate passed to his nephews and nieces.

19

Producer and Angel

The year is 1988 and I am taking a meeting (in Hollywood everyone 'takes' meetings) in John Daly's office at Hemdale Film Corporation on Beverly Boulevard in Los Angeles. Hemdale is riding high from the success of the first *Terminator* film and from winning Oscars for Best Picture in consecutive years for *Platoon* and *The Last Emperor*.

I have known John for many years from my time as a solicitor in London, when Hemdale was a tax-saving vehicle for some of the stars I represented. On the wall of his office is a signed photo taken at the Ali and Foreman 'Rumble in the Jungle' boxing match in Zaire which Hemdale promoted. We are meeting to work out the details of a joint venture in which I will be doing music supervision for Hemdale. It will be my job to source suitable background music for scenes with car radios, jukeboxes, nightclubs and the like. We have formed a company with the acronym STAMP, which I had intended to be Screen Television and Music Publishing, but because the name was not available we had to settle for 'Media' rather than 'Music'. STAMP will receive the revenues generated by the music when the films are distributed. John and I work out the details and agree the wording of a press release.

As it turns out the use of the word 'media' proves fortuitous. A few days later a small article about STAMP appears in *Variety*, the leading film newspaper in Hollywood. One person who reads the article is Len Mogel, the founder of *Heavy Metal* magazine – a science fiction monthly comic for adults. Len is interested in the media publishing aspect of STAMP as he is writing a book about all forms of media. When he gets in touch I have to tell him that the word 'media' only appears in the company name as second choice and that we are really a music publishing company for the film industry.

In any event we agree to meet for lunch the following day. I discover that Len is also one of the publishers of *National Lampoon*, a magazine that has lent its name to a number of successful movies including *Animal House* and *National Lampoon's Vacation*. We get to talking about film production, something that has always interested me. With his great knowledge of sci-fi publishing Len draws my attention to the author William Gibson, who established his name with the best-selling book *Neuromancer* a couple of years earlier. In it Gibson coined the terms cyberspace and cyberpunk; he envisioned the worldwide web years before it became a reality. *Neuromancer* was an award-winning novel set in Chiba city, an imagined virtual city in Japanese cyberspace. Its complexity and the numerous special effects required to transfer it to the medium of the cinema had been a deterrent to filmmakers.

However, Len has come across a short story by Gibson also set in cyberspace, which he says would be the perfect basis for a film. *Burning Chrome* is the name of the book. In the story Chrome is an evil megalomaniac intent on world domination. She seeks to control humanity by feeding addictive signals into everyone's brain cells. (The 'burning' of the title refers not to actual fire but a computer burn.) The story is also set in the futuristic landscape of Chiba City. It seems to me that Len is the perfect partner for a film project as he has several credits to his name, and I agree to join with him in investigating the potential of Gibson's story. We meet with Gibson's literary agent and take out an option to acquire the film rights to *Burning Chrome*. The option does not cost much, unless the project moves forward to the point where we decide to exercise it. We have a year to pick up the option.

The first essential element in getting a film financed is the treatment. This is a document outlining the storyline and characters. As the attention span of studio executives is notoriously short the treatment must be no more than a page in length, preferably less. If interest is shown a longer treatment can follow later, but with so many projects chasing so few sources of film finance the first step is the hardest. With Len's contacts we are able to get meetings at two major studios, 20th Century Fox and Universal, but the project is rejected by both on the grounds that it is too difficult to recreate cyberspace in film form without a huge budget for special effects. I mention the project to John Daly, although Hemdale is not known for big budget films. John is enthusiastic and encourages us to simplify the story so that it can be filmed without special effects, using exotic locations instead. As we have no other route to go down, we agree and the lawyers get to work on a production agreement with Hemdale.

As producers, Len and I get fees and points but nothing is to be paid until the film goes into production or, as they say, is 'greenlighted'. The definition of points has always been a bone of contention in Hollywood. Even points based on the film's gross can be made to disappear in the complexity of studio accounting. Net profit is to be avoided at all costs. The story is told of a screenwriter who was entitled to a large percentage of net profit of a hugely successful film that had made back its production costs several times over. The writer could get no satisfaction from the film's accountants so demanded a meeting with the producer Dino de Laurentiis.

He said to Dino: 'The movie has made huge profits around the world – where's my share of the net ?'

'Net?' Dino replied dismissively. 'Net is for fish.'

The next step is to find a director who meets with Hemdale's approval. We have selected Scott Roberts, a writer/director who gets to work on the screenplay. Scott produces five or six drafts, none of which prove acceptable to Hemdale. We take meetings with several other writers and directors. The chief problem is that the ones who are successful and in demand are not immediately available; there is always another project or two to be finished first. Our deal with Hemdale has a time limit on it. If the film does not go into production within two years, the property reverts back to Len and me, leaving Hemdale then out of the picture. As time goes by Hemdale runs into problems of its own, having financed a large number of total flops. So we are relieved when two years have gone by and once more we are able to start looking for a studio interested in making the film. Each year we have to make a payment to renew our option to acquire the film rights to the story.

In the meantime our author, William Gibson, has made a name for himself as the writer of the screenplay for *Aliens III*. He becomes the natural choice to work on a new screenplay for *Burning Chrome*. The director Kathryn Bigelow takes an interest in the project. This is a huge leap forward because she is married to James Cameron, the director of *Terminator* and *Rambo* films and a man who wields huge influence on getting a film into production. Through Kathryn we are introduced to Mario Kassar and Andy Vajna of Carolco, the most successful independent production studio in the world. Carolco is also home to James Cameron. We are told that Cameron will himself direct the film. This is fantastic news. Our deal with Carolco is signed, we are paid our producers' fees in full, and the option for the book is exercised. The only drawback is that the project is put on hold to wait for Cameron to finish his current project. It is decided that the film will be shot in Hong Kong and Japan to recreate Chiba City. I am sent off to Hong

Kong to scout locations. Before leaving I discover my UK passport is about to expire. When I come to complete the application for renewal it gives me a particular thrill to describe my occupation as 'film producer'.

For Chrome's headquarters I choose one of the most futuristic buildings in the world, housing the Hong Kong and Shanghai Bank; for the slums of Chiba City, the hugely over-crowded boat people of Aberdeen harbour are perfect. Mean-while another screenplay which our author has written, also set in cyberspace, is released as the film *Johnny Mnemonic*. This film proves to be a flop at the box office. Carolco debates the commercial risk that might be attached to another cyberspace film and Cameron starts work on another film, pushing our project further back by at least a year. Then in 1995, seven years into the project, disaster strikes; Carolco suddenly goes out of business and into some form of liquidation. The assets of Carolco, including the rights to *Burning Chrome*, are sold to a French film company.

And that is the last we hear of the project. In spite of several greenlights, dozens of screenplays written, hundreds of meetings taken, and thousands of phone calls made, in the end the film fails to make it into production. Ah well. At least we were film producers for a while and were paid accordingly.

The lure of show business is still there and I decide to get involved with a Broadway play. A friend of Denny Cordell from Ireland, Sean Beary, approaches us as potential investors in a play called *K2* by a new playwright, Patrick Meyers. The entire action of the play is set on an icy ledge somewhere near the summit of K2, the second-highest mountain in the world. There are only two characters in the play, climbers on their descent from the summit. One has fallen and broken a leg. The other must decide either to risk death and wait until a search party finds them or to abandon his best friend to an icy death and descend by himself. The set is so realistic that five tons of snow and ice are brought to the theatre each night. The audience in the front rows have to be protected by plastic sheeting from the snow blowing off the stage.

The idea seems so original and the drama so exciting that we write our cheques and become credited as co-producers, or 'angels'. Naturally we want two seasoned actors with box office appeal for the roles of the two climbers. The senior producer who makes the decisions cannot wait for two big names to become available and the play opens with two fine actors with lesser-known names. There is another drawback; the author refuses to allow the play to be performed with an interval because he believes it will break the suspense. This means the audience must sit still for three hours without a break. Those in the front stalls slowly freeze, no doubt dreaming of the appearance of a St Bernard bearing brandy. The rest have to wait patiently for a smoke, a drink or a trip to the toilets.

After opening night, in the tradition of Broadway, we repair to Sardi's restaurant to await the early editions of the papers. We munch on Sardi's celebrated strawberry shortcake while anxiously awaiting the reviews. On the whole they are good. The icy set comes in for special praise and later gathers a Tony for best stage set. Not soon enough, however. The award when it comes is rather like a medal awarded posthumously. For a few weeks *K2* plays to full houses but slowly the audience drops away, partly I think because the cast are not well-known enough and partly because the word of mouth about the lack of an interval is putting people off. The harrowing content and unhappy ending might also be a factor. The play definitely does not offer a feel-good experience. It runs for three and a half months, nothing like long enough to get its money back for the investors.

I put it down as an interesting but expensive experience. In gambling terms, backing a stage play must be regarded as extremely high-risk. For the author, however, things eventually turn out very well. A film of the play gets made in 1990, directed by Franc Roddam. This results in a tiny dividend being paid to the producers of the play, though not enough to make an appreciable dent in our overall loss.

20

O. J. Simpson

Timing is everything in life and my venture into the pre-paid telephone card business could not have happened at a worse time since Alexander Graham Bell first invented the telephone.

My partner in this ill-fated project was a colourful character called Donald Brown. We met by chance at Los Angeles Airport in early 1994. He was returning from Atlanta where he had been for Super Bowl XXVIII and I was on my way back from a business trip to Seattle. There was a long queue for taxis at the airport and as he was standing next to me in the line we agreed to share. He lived in Santa Monica which was on the way to my home in Beverly Hills. During the drive back he told me he went to the Super Bowl every year thanks to tickets supplied by O. J. Simpson. At that time O.J. was one of the best-known and most well-liked personalities in the United States. Not only was he one of the greatest American footballers of all time but he had made the transition to movie star with parts in such blockbusters as *The Towering Inferno* and *The Naked Gun*. He had several important and lucrative endorsement deals and was often to be seen sprinting through airports in TV commercials for Hertz car rentals.

Don Brown is best described as a likeable rogue. Originally from Ireland, he became a minor player in a scam operated at JFK Airport in the 1960s which resulted in certain shipments of illegal substances being imported without official inspection. His part in this activity is mentioned in Howard Marks' biography *Mr Nice*. As I travel on an Irish passport this gave us something in common and we soon became friends. He confided in me that he had spent two years in a Federal prison for his part in the scam.

Don was a bull of man with a shock of wavy red hair and he was certainly tough enough to serve his time without too many problems. While he was there he befriended a weaker prisoner who was being given a rough time by one of the prison gangs and saved him from further hard treatment. This man turned out to be a distant relative of O.J. and as a consequence ever since his release from prison Don had received Super Bowl tickets from O.J.

The losing team in Super Bowl XXVIII was O.J.'s old team the Buffalo Bills, which meant O.J. was very much in evidence in Atlanta. Don had spent some time with O.J. in the days before the game and as a result now had what he described as the greatest opportunity in his life to make some real money legally. He told me that O.J. had agreed to give him the exclusive rights to use his name and photograph on pre-paid phone cards. I knew next to nothing about phone cards but Don made it sound interesting enough for me to agree to meet him for lunch in Santa Monica later that week.

Phone cards are still in use across the world, but in wealthier countries they have had to give way to mobile phones. Back then phone cards sold in their millions. Southern California was a huge market because of the large immigrant population, both legal and illegal, many of whom did not have a telephone in their home. As a more convenient alternative to using a pocketful of quarters at a payphone, cards could be bought at any five-and-dime store, seven-eleven, airport or bus station, and these were valid on any payphone or landline. Sold in denominations of $5 or $10, cards provided the corresponding value in minutes of talktime. The proceeds of sales were split between the card company, the phone company as service provider, and the retailer.

The instructions on using the card, the numbers to call and the PIN number for that card were all found on one side. The other side of the card was pictorial. It might be a view of Golden Gate Bridge, an abstract design, or the face of a minor celebrity. As yet no one as well known as O.J. had given his name and image to a phone card.

The following week I had lunch with Don in his local Santa Monica coffee shop. When I arrived he was joking around with the waitresses and making them laugh. As I got to know him I saw that there were two sides to his character. Most of the time he used his Irish charm and gift of the gab to get what he wanted, and he often succeeded in charming the most unlikely people. However, he had a short fuse and if things did not go his way might explode with rage. He had on occasion become so abusive that there were people who refused to deal with him.

By the time we met Don had a deal memo signed by O.J.'s agent, giving Don the exclusive rights to produce phone cards with O.J.'s image printed on them. For these rights O.J. was to receive an advance of $20,000, a much smaller sum than he was used to getting for use of his name. The problem was money, or rather the lack of it. Don had none and the banks would not lend money to a convicted felon. Don needed a partner and with expansive details of the fortune we were about to reap he convinced me that I should invest. We set up a company, rented an office and planned the design and distribution of the cards. As well as providing several photos we could use, O.J. had agreed to record a short message so that when the card was used the caller heard O.J. say, 'You are connected with the Juice.'

It took us a while to find a phone company with a switch

large enough to handle the huge volume of calls that we anticipated as soon as the cards were on the market. Display stands featuring a life-size mock-up of O.J. in cardboard were made. Orders started pouring in and before long we placed orders for hundreds of thousands of cards to be manufactured. Expenses mounted but we were confident of being about to make a killing.

We started shipping out boxes of cards to retailers and distributors at the beginning of June 1994. All seemed set fair and I was already working out how much profit we would make. Then on 12 June the shocking news came through that O.J.'s ex-wife Nicole and her friend Ronald Goldman had been found murdered outside her apartment in Los Angeles. It did not take the LA Police Department long to decide to charge O.J. with both murders. I was in London at the time and saw no real reason to worry as I did not think that the publicity, adverse as it was, would slow the sale of phone cards. I had always believed that any publicity was better than none. I could not have been more wrong.

O.J.'s lawyers had agreed with the Los Angeles Police Department that O.J. would turn himself in on 17 June and make a statement to the press. When he failed to show up an all-points arrest warrant was issued by the police. Eventually O.J. was spotted being driven down the freeway as a passenger in his friend Al Cowling's white Ford Bronco. O.J. was said to be holding a pistol to his head and threatening to shoot himself as the police cars followed the Bronco around the LA freeway system. All of this was seen live on TV. All channels broke into their scheduled programming to show the slow-speed chase. Finally O.J. surrendered and was taken into custody. He was now the most famous, or infamous, person in the United States.

Don Brown was not someone to let any promotional opportunity slip. There was a trade show in Los Angeles where he had taken a stand to sell the phone cards. As he knew Al Cowling he arranged to borrow the white Bronco and put it on the stand at the trade show. He even had some phone cards printed with the white Bronco on them. It attracted a lot of attention but probably did little to help promote the cards as public opinion was turning sharply against O.J. Most people thought his actions were those of a guilty man. Within a few days we started getting returns from distributors. Soon abusive phone calls followed and people asked why we were working with a murderer. Retailers complained that customers were threatening to stay away from their stores until they got rid of the O.J. cards on display. The trickle of returns became an avalanche and the office was soon stacked to the ceiling with boxes of unsaleable phone cards.

Although O.J. was subsequently found not guilty in the murder trial, he became a social outcast and the market for O.J. phone cards never recovered. Taking into account O.J.'s advance, the cost of producing the cards and the display packaging, the rent of the office and the deposit paid to the telephone company, the whole exercise cost me a small fortune. Yet had we done the same thing a year earlier, there's every reason to believe we could have made a much bigger one.

Don Brown was not a man to give up easily and together we had a couple more tries at the phone card business. At O.J.'s trial evidence was given of his abusive behaviour towards his wife Nicole Brown Simpson and the beatings she received from him. Nicole's sister Denise Brown started a charitable foundation in Nicole's memory with the object of helping victims of domestic violence which she promoted with the slogan 'No Excuse for Abuse'. Don made a deal with her to produce No Excuse phone cards from which some small part of the profit would be paid to the foundation.

How he managed to talk her into working with the same company that had promoted O.J. is a testament to Don's power of persuasion. The cards carrying the 'No Excuse for Abuse' message were bright pink and distributed in ladies' hairdressers, beauty salons and fashion stores. Sadly, sales were dismal. We had not calculated that the type of person who frequented these establishments did not fit the profile of a phone card user. We chalked up another loss. Then Don had a brainwave – an inspiration that would supposedly recoup all our losses and put us a long way in front.

By this time – somewhat late in the day – we knew that the real market for cards was to be found in the poorer, largely Hispanic, section of the population. Many of these people had left families behind in Mexico with whom they wanted to keep in touch. Don's idea was to produce a card that could be used both in the US and in Mexico. But what image were we to put on the cards to attract Mexican users? This was to be Don's masterstroke.

The Virgin of Guadalupe is Mexico's most beloved religious icon and cultural image. Since the War of Independence it has come to symbolize the Mexican nation. It is the most holy shrine in Mexico and the Virgin's anniversary is a national holiday. The popular image of the Virgin is over 500 years old and is familiar to every Mexican. Don somehow managed to persuade the Bishop of Guadalupe, whose cathedral is home to the shrine, to meet with him. At the meeting he sold the idea of a Virgin phone card to the Bishop. No doubt the Bishop was swayed by talk of the millions of dollars that the cards would raise for the Church. Then Don pulled off his great publicity coup. He made a giant mock-up of the card with an image of the Virgin of Guadalupe on it and persuaded the Bishop to bless the four-foot-high card in the cathedral. The next day every newspaper in Mexico carried a picture of the blessing of the card. Surely this time we would sell cards by the million.

We had made a deal with a Mexican telephone company to provide the phone time and distribute the cards. Demand was high and sales rocketed. The company had agreed to send us monthly statements of sales together with our share of the proceeds. A month or two went by without any statement. Don began calling the company in Mexico every day without any result. Each day he became more and more angry.

Being hot-tempered and impulsive, Don found it impossible to stay calm and resolve the situation rationally, if that was ever possible. After getting nowhere on the phone, he took a flight to Mexico City. Once there, having already fortified himself with several large drinks on the flight, he stormed into the company's offices. Bellowing and cursing at everyone he encountered, he threatened to rip the throats out of the management if he didn't get his royalty payments there and then. The police were called in and Don was put on a flight back to LA.

We were now at war with the Mexicans. They had a battery of lawyers who raised every kind of legal objection to our agreement. Our only recourse was to file a lawsuit in Mexico City which was both expensive and time consuming. The phone company's lawyers managed to stall the situation for well over a year, by which time demand for the cards had diminished. The end came when the company closed its doors and went into liquidation. We received precisely nothing. For me it was the final blow. I had to swallow my losses and say farewell to phone cards for good. Sad to say, Don never got over the fact that a fortune that had been almost in his grasp had slipped through his fingers. He died of a heart attack a couple of years later.

More recently I learned about another publicity coup, excelling even Don's card blessing in the cathedral. In Monaco I met an Australian stockbroker who told me the following story.

Some years ago, when Australian mining shares were all the rage, the brokers – let us call them Smith and Brown – wanted to publicise a mining issue they were promoting. They decided to place a half-page ad in the *Sydney Morning Herald*. Regulations prevented them from pushing the shares in the advertisement, so the wording they used went like this:

– chauffeuse wanted for partners' Rolls-Royce
– must be under 30, slim and blonde
– previous experience unnecessary
– apply Smith and Brown, etc. etc.

The advertisement duly appeared and was met with a storm of protest from feminist groups, the Australian stock exchange and other brokers. The furore was so great that Smith and Brown were interviewed on national television and the story appeared in newspapers and magazines across the country. The authorities could not censure them because all they had done was advertise a job vacancy. Naturally, when interviewed they took every opportunity to ramp up the shares in the mining company and in the process acquired a slew of new clients. All in all, a very prosperous time was enjoyed by Smith and Brown.

Some years went by and the stock market was going through a slow patch. Smith and Brown decided it was time to place another advertisement. This time they took a full page in the newspaper. The top half consisted of three words in huge block capitals: WE ARE BACK! Beneath this ran wording almost identical to that of the first ad, but with two minor changes:

– pilot wanted for partners' helicopter
– must be under 30, slim and blonde

– previous experience unnecessary
– apply Smith and Brown, etc. etc.

This time the ad elevated Smith and Brown to the status of folk heroes. It brought them so much business that within a few years they were able to retire to Monaco.

21

Ireland

In his autobiography Ronnie Wood refers to Sandymount, his estate in Ireland, as his sanctuary and says there is nowhere better than the Emerald Isle. It was at Sandymount that I spent the greatest amount of time with Ronnie and the adventures we shared were legion. Curiously my name is not mentioned in connection with Ireland during the time after Ronnie bought Sandymount in 1990 until we parted company twelve years later. It is as if I had been airbrushed out of the picture.

With parents who were born and buried in Dublin and having spent all my childhood holidays with my grandmother in Rathmines, I regard Dublin as my spiritual home and I travel on an Irish passport. From the moment I met Ronnie I always thought that life in Ireland would appeal to him.

By 1990 Denny Cordell was firmly established as a racehorse trainer in County Kildare. Whenever I came over from Los Angeles I stayed with him at his house deep in the heart of the Irish countryside. On one such visit Denny suggested that I invite the Woods to stay for the weekend. Ronnie was all for it but Josephine, his wife, was not too keen to go to Ireland. When I asked her why not she replied 'Because I've never been there.' I managed to persuade her to come and the weekend stretched into one and then three weeks, with the Woods' children coming over to join us. In a word, they fell in love with Ireland and asked me to find them a house. Jonathan Irwin, an old school pal of mine, had a house for sale where I had often stayed for the Irish Derby. I thought it would be perfect for the Woods. They agreed and the agreement to purchase was struck the very first day they saw the house. Much work was done to build recording and art studios in the buildings adjoining the house, together with a pub and snooker room. A year later a pool house was added complete with jacuzzi, which was kept heated to tropical temperature throughout the year. Sandymount became my home from home and I was often there for weeks at a time.

Josephine, who always went on tour with Ronnie and rarely let him out of her sight, even allowed us to spend time together at Sandymount while she stayed in London. We had a high old time on our frequent excursions into Dublin at night. Our schedule was always the same. After a day spent in Ronnie's pub at Sandymount watching the racing and having a few bets I would cook a light meal, usually chicken soup, after which we would head out for Dublin. First stop was the Horseshoe Bar in the Shelburne Hotel, where most evenings there was a regular turnover of prominent figures, from the editor of the *Irish Times* to the latest fashion icons.

Well refreshed, we moved on to Reynard's, a bar always staffed by some lovely Irish lasses. Next stop was Lily's Bordello, Dublin's liveliest club where we settled ourselves in the VIP room for a few hours, sometimes in the company of Bono and the Edge from U2 and always with an interesting crowd. Lily's closed around 3 a.m. by which time we had usually gathered a group around us who were ready to party all night. The after-hours bars which stayed open until dawn were in Leeson Street where we could be found until first light. Then it was back to Sandymount with assorted stragglers for drinks, swimming, the jacuzzi and whatever else was on offer. Needless to say, we rarely came back on our own. The girls were sent back to Dublin in the afternoon.

There was one problem with Sandymount. Beautiful as the

land around the house was, it belonged to the neighbouring farmer, apart from a small acreage immediately around the house, and privacy was therefore limited. I entered into negotiations with the farmer that were to take three years to bring to a conclusion. These were not productive of much in the way of entertainment. For a start he was one of the few Irishmen who never drank alcohol. On top of that he had no sense of humour. Worst of all, he had a chip on his shoulder about Ronnie living in Sandymount because it was the house he had been brought up in as a boy. His father, also a farmer, had sold off the big house years before in order to keep all the land. After three years and countless cups of tea I managed to persuade the farmer to sell another sixty acres around Sandymount. He made Ronnie pay double the going rate for land at that time but Ronnie had the last laugh because over the next few years the Celtic Tiger roared and the value of land doubled and redoubled more than once. Sandymount is now one of the finest small Georgian estates within an hour of Dublin and worth many millions of pounds.

Many of rock 'n' roll's greatest came to record at the studio at Sandymount. Among them was Bob Dylan, who had built up a portfolio of valuable property in New York, and who asked me to find him a similar house in Ireland. Such properties were hard to come by and by the time I found something suitable prices had risen considerably. Bob decided they had gone too high and did not proceed, though had he known the extraordinary levels that property prices would reach in Ireland over the next few years he might have decided differently.

It was in his studio in Ireland that Ronnie recorded his solo album 'Slide On This' in 1992. Although Ronnie had made some critically acclaimed albums in the past, they had not sold well enough to make money for the record labels. He was not alone in this situation – even Mick couldn't make a financial success of solo recording. I had a difficult job finding a label to cover the cost of 'Slide On This' until I came across a new label, Continuum, which was willing to pay for the prestige of having a Rolling Stone on the roster of artists. I got them to agree to put up $400,000 for the album and to pay for some tour support to promote it. Many all-night sessions were spent in the studio as numerous guest artists put in appearances including Charlie Watts, the Edge and Jeff Beck.

The making of a studio album is akin to making a film with a director who shoots every scene dozens of times until he is satisfied. Repetition is the name of the game. On average an album has 14 tracks which may have been whittled down from perhaps twice as many. After one hundred or so nights in the studio each track has been worked and played back dozens of times, each with a minor variation – some more guitar here, less bass there, and so on. I was present for many of those nights in the studio while the album was being completed, sometimes falling asleep even with playback at high volume, such was the tedium of the recording process. It was all right for the musicians because they could sleep it off the next day, but I had an office to run and had to be up in the daytime to make telephone calls and go into Dublin for meetings.

After the album's release a tour of the US by the Ronnie Wood band was put together. I was to spend six weeks literally on the road as this tour, in total contrast with Stones tours, was a low-budget affair involving travel by bus. After an opening show in New York we set off for the first stop in Atlanta. I rode with the seven band members and Jo Wood in the first bus, while the tour manager, roadie, sound equipment and lighting followed in bus number two. We travelled round the entire US – down to Florida, across to New Orleans and Texas, then up the West Coast from Los Angeles to Seattle.

Many a time I had to cancel interviews because Ronnie had partyed too hard the night before and could not get himself ready for the press. However, no show was ever delayed or cancelled and we completed the circuit through Canada and back down to New England to finish in Boston six weeks after setting out.

Just about every member of every band started life on the road the hard way – unless born into an already successful group such as the Jacksons. Before fame and fortune arrived, travel from gig to gig was by dilapidated van with every band member taking a turn at the wheel. They carried their own equipment and did everything for themselves until they could afford a roadie. Everything changed once a record deal was signed and the band saw the magic words 'tour support' in their contract. Tour support meant that the record label made up the shortfall between the cost of touring and the proceeds of gigs.

When the Rolling Stones perform in a 50,000-seater stadium the gross take from seat and merchandise sales is around $3 million. After paying for the rent of the venue and all other costs including the crew, entourage and staging there is still a huge profit to be made. When bands are less well-known and the venues get progressively smaller the profit margin reduces rapidly to the point where the cost of putting on the show plus travel expenses exceeds the income from ticket and merchandise sales. But touring is important not only for getting the band's name in front of a live audience but also for local publicity. Press and local radio interviews will be arranged in every town in which the band performs.

Even for a relatively small band to go on tour the expenses are high. Before any tour takes to the road there will be several weeks of rehearsals for the band to work out which songs they will perform, who will take solos and when, and every other detail of the performance. The band must be accommodated in one place near the rehearsal hall while this takes place. The sound and lighting equipment will be tested during rehearsals. Lead vocalists tend to be prima donnas and won't settle for anything less than a suite, even if it has to be in a Holiday Inn rather than a Four Seasons Hotel. To go to a radio station for an on-the-air interview they will insist on travelling by limo. In addition to the band members there will be a tour manager, a sound man and a lighting technician, and at least one roadie to help with loading and unloading the gear. Bands take their own sound and light equipment on the road because the house equipment varies so much from venue to venue.

Then there is the expense of feeding and housing the whole party. Each individual receives a sum of money every day – the 'per diem' – to cover food, drink and extras such as hotel telephone calls. The tour manager has many jobs, from dealing with the promoter to ensure the band receives its proper cut of the gate, to scheduling the arrival and departure times and paying the hotel bills.

Even for the smallest of tours there is a quantity of heavy equipment to be moved around and the cheapest way of moving a dozen or so people around plus their gear is by bus. Tour buses are fitted out with lounges, video/audio equipment and even with bunks for travel by night. When the Ronnie Wood Band embarked on a six-week tour of the United States by bus it was in sharp contrast to the style of travel the musicians had been used to, and Ronnie in particular was highly sceptical, but after a few days on the road a routine was established with which everyone seemed happy. The band performed about four times a week. On a travel day the band members piled into the first bus immediately after the close of the show. The others loaded the equipment onto the second bus and followed an hour or two later.

On board the bus, with the band still on an adrenaline high

from their performance, drinks flowed freely while a videotape of the evening's show was played. Much discussion took place comparing one night with another and deciding what changes should be made for the next show. The bunks on the bus were rarely used, except by me as I had to be awake enough the following day to call the record company and arrange press interviews and radio station visits. We would arrive at a modest hotel in the early hours of the morning having travelled a few hundred miles. Once or twice a week there would be a rest day; on other days there was a show to prepare for, involving a sound check in the afternoon. The size of venue varied from place to place. Sometimes it would be in a theatre seating a thousand or more; or it might be a club with a capacity of a few hundred. If ticket sales were going slowly I would have to get Ronnie to the local radio station to be interviewed on air. Tickets would be given away to the first few callers to the station. Bearing in mind that the main objective of touring is to promote and sell an album, air play at the radio station was the key to success and to ensure the new album gets played the artist must visit the radio station to be interviewed in person. It's hard work for the artist as the same questions will be asked time and time again from city to city.

Ireland remained the focal point for Ronnie's musical activities for a few years until, after the Stones 'Voodoo Lounge' tour, the Woods moved from their house in Richmond to a huge pile on Kingston Hill which had once been a gift from the nation to Queen Victoria on her engagement to Albert. Josephine persuaded Ronnie to build another recording studio at this house in order to spend less time in Ireland. I was having a hard time controlling the outflow of money and thought this an unnecessary expense. It was a complicated and expensive engineering project involving the excavation and construction of an underground space to contain the studio. Thereafter our trips to Ireland became less frequent and Ronnie's last solo album was recorded in London.

Containing the outward flow of money was an increasingly difficult problem. Jo was wildly extravagant and setting any kind of budget was a hopeless task. The pool house in Ireland ended up costing more than Sandymount, a six-bedroom Georgian manor house and grounds. When the house on Kingston Hill was purchased, Jo told me that it needed nothing doing to it. Actually a builder was engaged full-time for several years at a cost of millions. Racks of clothes arrived on a regular basis and huge sums were spent on holidays and birthdays. All of this money came from Ronnie's earnings as a musician. In addition he supported most of Jo's family on a regular basis. As the one who had to sign the cheques, I was bound to spend much of my time trying to curb the worst excesses.

The time came when Ronnie asked me to find a project which would keep Josephine in London while we could spend time in Ireland. This resulted in the ill-fated Harrington private members' club in South Kensington, which lost Ronnie and myself millions of pounds as well as costing me my job as manager. Like most projects, it was started with the best of intentions and an affordable budget. Members' club were in vogue and the Harrington had the added attraction of a spa which we thought would be popular in that part of London. Once Josephine became involved in the design, the budget flew out the window and the costs escalated out of control. After several years of construction I felt we could not abandon the project as so much time and money had gone into it. It was as though a savage dog had sunk its teeth into my leg; it was extremely painful but I could not shake it off for fear of bleeding to death.

When the club eventually opened Josephine insisted that it

should be very expensive and ultra-exclusive. We even made Rod Stewart pay for a membership. In fact it was so exclusive that it lost money from the opening day and within a year I was out of a job and removed from the project. My successor, Josephine's son, fell out with our partner in the project almost immediately and resorted to legal proceedings, and this in my view cost Ronnie another pile of money.

Some Girls

'Some Girls' is the title of one of the best regarded studio albums by the Rolling Stones. Released in 1968, the title song reflects on the virtues and vices of girls of different nationalities and races. Here is my take on some girls who have passed my way to a greater or lesser degree.

I begin with Julie Christie because she was the most strikingly beautiful girl I have ever met. Not only was she blessed with extraordinary hypnotic eyes and a sensuous mouth but she exuded a kind of louche awareness that epitomised the early '60s. In 1961 I was a law student living with my parents in Kensington. A good friend, Gerald, lived nearby in a flat with a couple of other guys. He was lucky enough to be Julie's boyfriend at the time. I used to visit him frequently and often saw Julie at the flat. Her looks set her apart from the other girls we used to take to the local pub. She was then an almost unknown twenty-year old actress. I was full of admiration when she landed a part in the TV series *A for Andromeda* as she was the first person I had met who was in the public eye. She went on to take the lead role in *Darling* for which she received the best actress Oscar.

Brilliant as she was in *Doctor Zhivago*, I can never watch that film without thinking back to my twenty-first birthday. My parents gave me a cocktail party at which Gerald and Julie were amongst the guests. I was quite naïve in matters of relationships and had never discussed anything of a sexual nature with my parents. I suffered acute embarrassment when, in front of my mother, I heard Julie ask Gerald to get her a glass of champagne, to which he replied, 'All you girls ever want is liquid in one orifice or another.' I could not look at her in quite the same light again, even in her film roles, without remembering that remark. After Julie and Gerald split up I never had occasion to meet her again.

Lynn Redgrave was someone with whom I had a much more enduring friendship. I met her husband-to-be, John Clark, in 1967 when he came to my office for some legal advice shortly after I had inherited the law firm from David Jacobs. Lynn and John soon became good friends with me and my wife Caroline. To some extent our lives were in parallel, in that we got married around the same time and each had two children, a girl and a boy. We were regular dinner guests at each other's houses in London and we both moved to California at different times in our lives. Although Lynn had achieved international fame with the film *Georgy Girl* at a very early age, she remained totally unspoilt and down-to-earth. She was especially kind to our old nanny who was looking after a third generation of Cowan children. She and Caroline would walk their dogs on Barnes Common and swap recipes. John and I loved our food and the girls were both great cooks. Diets were high on the list of topics of conversation as we all tended to put on weight. Lynn finally laid that to rest when she became the international spokesperson for Weightwatchers. Lynn was a great party giver and had an interesting circle of theatrical friends. She once brought the actor Sir John Mills to our house for dinner. He outstayed and out-drank everyone and I had the greatest difficulty getting him into a taxi to take him home. Her culinary tour de force, which often appeared at her parties, was the best kedgeree I have ever eaten.

In common with many people, John had an aversion to paying lawyers' fees. He often consulted me unofficially on legal matters but was more inclined to be his own lawyer. Armed with a library of do-it-yourself books on the law he decided to save a few hundred pounds and act for himself when he and Lynn sold their house in Barnes. Something went wrong at the time of completion and he made the error of allowing the buyer to move in before the house had been paid for. Soon there were delays with the money and excuses for non-payment. It took many months of legal wrangling for the situation to be resolved. Over the years John has become something of a legal eagle and has been involved in some very extended litigation, notably when he and Lynn established the right for a mother to breast-feed a child on the set of a film. More recently John has been representing himself in a series of actions against Lynn following their much-publicised split in 1997.

Another actress who was briefly my client when I first took over the entertainment law firm after David Jacobs' death was Marsha Hunt, who played the part of Dionne in the first London production of *Hair* in 1968. She was perfect for the part as she had an enormous halo of bushy hair enveloping her head. After the opening night of *Hair* Marsha posed nude for the photographer Patrick Lichfield and the resulting photograph appeared on the cover of *Vogue*. I was later to learn from my own experience that Marsha was not shy. During the run of *Hair* there was an accident on stage with some explosive material which resulted in her being burned in the middle of her back. I was consulted to advise on the claim that could be made against the insurers of the production. I advised Marsha that she should see a specialist and that I would need medical reports to get counsel's opinion on the damages she might seek. To my surprise Marsha invited me round to her flat to inspect the damage. Curiosity got the better of me and one evening I found myself in her flat for the examination. Although it was not strictly necessary, Marsha bared her upper torso in all its glory so that I could view the burn. She had a wonderful body with perfect breasts and I might have been tempted to try my luck had not a couple of her friends arrived at the crucial moment. Somehow they seemed to think it an enormous joke to find me in my pin-stripe suit, stiff collar and old school tie with a half-naked Marsha. The case never came to court because the burn healed up and the producers paid Marsha's medical bills.

Persis Khambatta was at least the equal in looks to any girl I have encountered. She became Miss India when she was only fifteen and took part in a number of beauty pageants before appearing in some Bollywood films in which she had minor roles. I first met her in London shortly before I gave up practising law and moved to Los Angeles. She was relatively unknown until she landed the part of Lieutenant Ilea in *Star Trek*, for which she shaved her head. She was seen by an audience of millions when she presented an award at the 1979 Oscars. I took her out several times in Los Angeles and we had a brief fling. Her unique appearance caused heads to turn wherever we went. We went to a fancy dress Hallowe'en party in role reversal; she dressed as a man in suit and tie and I donned a dark wig and staggered around in heels looking like Peter Sellers' sister. She had a very sweet and caring nature and was a constant supporter of Mother Teresa, to whom she donated the royalties from her book *Pride of India*. She had a serious car crash in the early eighties from which she never properly recovered, and died of a heart attack when she was only forty-nine.

In complete contrast to these lovely people, in 1994, when I had been living in Monaco for some years, I met a female of a very different character. The line in Rudyard Kipling's poem, 'The female of the species is more deadly than the male', comes to mind. I went for a drink one evening to the American Bar at the Hotel de Paris and got into conversation with an attractive lady whom I took to be in her thirties. I was later to discover that she was forty-six years old. She told me that her name was Jamila and that she was living in Cannes. She said she was thinking of moving to Monaco and questioned me on the pros and cons of living there. I found her entertaining and arranged to have lunch with her the next day. To my surprise she told me she was the Countess of Shaftesbury. I knew of the Earl of Shaftesbury, whose title goes back to the time of King Charles II, in connection with his extensive estate at Wimborne St Giles in Dorset. I had never met the Earl but it seemed an unlikely match as Jamila was clearly of North African extraction and was more at home speaking French than English. I was curious to discover how she had married into one of the oldest titled families in England. She said her husband had given her a present of a villa in Cannes and a chateau in Versailles. The villa was real but I later discovered that the chateau belonged to the Earl and he had promised her the very valuable contents of antiques. She produced some documents she had received from a solicitor from which it appeared that Anthony Ashley Cooper, the 10th Earl of Shaftesbury, wanted to transfer an estate in Northern Ireland to her. It all seemed extraordinary. She asked for my advice on the papers. I told her that she must consult a solicitor herself as I had long ago given up practising law and my knowledge was very out of date.

I saw her again a few weeks later when she came to Monaco with her sister who lived in Switzerland. She then confessed that she was separated from her husband and had not seen him for months. I invited the two of them to stay at my apartment for a couple of days. The sisters dressed only in designer clothes and were fully equipped with the Cote d'Azur accessories of Chanel sunglasses, Hermès handbags and Versace beach towels. Since they were clearly in Monaco looking for fun I did not question their provenance. A friend of mine joined us for a night on the town in Monaco and after a long night of dancing and drinking at Sass café I ended up spending the night with Jamila. I saw her once more when I went over to her luxurious villa in the exclusive Californie district of Cannes where she was living in great style. No more was said about a move to Monaco.

A few months later in November 2004 it was reported in the press that the Earl of Shaftesbury was missing. Much was made of the fact that he had fallen into a life of drink, drugs and prostitutes. He had last been seen in some seedy bars in the red light district of Cannes. When no trace of the Earl was found after several weeks of extensive enquiries, I read that Jamila M'barek, as she was called before her marriage, was a former escort. She and her brother had been called in for questioning by the French police. After lengthy interrogation Jamila admitted that her brother had killed the Earl accidentally in a drunken fight following a meeting to discuss Jamila's divorce settlement on 5 November 2004. The Earl had earlier announced his intention to marry another younger escort girl. It was not until several months later that the Earl's body was found in a remote ravine in the Alpes Maritimes.

Jamila and her brother were charged with murder. The police had bugged a conversation between Jamila and her sister in which it was said that Jamila had paid her brother €140,000 to kill her husband. Jamila had stood to inherit another fortune under the Earl's will but that will would have been made void in the event of their divorce. After a four-day trial in Nice

Jamila and her brother Mohammed were convicted of murder in May 2007 and sentenced to 25 years each. For me it was an eerie feeling to have known an evil murderess a short time before she had her husband killed. During the trial the Earl's current mistress, another escort, gave evidence to the effect that the Earl wanted to marry her. She said that she loved him very much, adding 'He was like a cash machine.' I think that says it all.

23

Sex, Drugs and Rock 'n' Roll

I was lucky enough to be involved in the music business when rock 'n' roll was sweeping the world. Looking back at some of the rock heroes whose paths I have crossed in the past 30 years, it's easy enough to conclude that the music really arises out of a mix of sex, drugs and alcohol. From the Beatles' gentle 'I Wanna Hold Your Hand' to the Stones' blatant 'Let's Spend The Night Together', rock has always been about sex. Throw in a plentiful supply of drugs and alcohol and you have the perfect ingredients for creating rock music.

To a greater or lesser degree the rock stars of the '50s and '60s fuelled their creativity with an excess of groupies, vodka and cocaine. The most memorable rock anthems were composed in alcoholic, drug-fuelled binges. From Jerry Lee Lewis and Chuck Berry in the US to Jagger/Richards and Stewart/Wood in Britain the best of their greatest hits came in these early years. As they grew older and wiser and began to reign in the early excesses, the creative stream began to dry up. It was as if the drugs and alcohol were the rocket fuel necessary to keep the creative juices flowing. Who can remember a Stones song written in the last twenty years? Why has Rod Stewart turned to the great songwriters of Broadway for his more recent albums? Why is Jerry Lee Lewis still pounding out 'Great Balls Of Fire' and Chuck Berry calling long-distance information? It's the early compositions that audiences still want to hear.

The availability of sex was greatly enhanced by the arrival of the pill and the 'make love, not war' movement that followed. A story told me by Ronnie Wood well conveys the flavour of that era. When he was young and on tour with the Jeff Beck band, of which Rod Stewart was the vocalist, he and Rod would dress up as doctors in surgical gowns. The security men or roadies would send a girl up to their room, telling her 'The doctor will see you now.' She would then be stripped and given a thorough examination, complete with tut-tutting and 'Oohh! You must have a look at this' exchanges between Rod and Ronnie. This prank was repeated on many occasions.

Being on the road was an opportunity to get away from wives and girlfriends. Bill Wyman is reputed to have slept with thousands of women, though on Stones tours he was not one for participating in the cocaine and alcohol sessions enjoyed by Keith and Ronnie. Jerry Hall put up with Mick's widely reported dalliances for many years until, as Jo Wood told me, he brought back a dose of a sexual disease from the Cannes film festival. Unlike Jo who was on tour the entire time, Jerry used to appear only from time to time in the major cities like London, New York and Paris and she usually brought children with her. I found her charming, easy to talk to and very friendly. She would ask after my children and had a smile for everyone. When she had her chat show on TV I met with her to arrange a feature on Ronnie's art and found her very helpful.

The following story was told to me by one of Jerry's best friends, Lady Rose Musker (formerly Lambton), also a great friend of mine. Rose is one of the five daughters of the late Lord Lambton, who had to resign from the government after an affair with a call girl, Norma Levy. Rose and Jerry were talking with a couple of other women friends about the men in their life. At one point they asked who was the oldest man each had slept with – one said when she was twenty she had a boyfriend of forty, another when thirty a man twenty-five years older and so on. When it came to Jerry to speak she turned to Rose and said in her Texan drawl, 'Your daddy!'

It wasn't only the stars who enjoyed limitless sex. Lower down the ladder the roadies and sidemen could help themselves from the hordes of girls who hung around hotel lobbies hoping to get close to a band on the road. In Tokyo I witnessed aspirins being distributed to groups of girls who believed they were being given birth control pills before they were allowed upstairs. It is the security men who call the shots as to who gets backstage or who can go up from a hotel lobby to the band's floors, and they are in the best position to get favours from girls who want to meet musicians. On a Stones tour each band member has his own personal security man. In addition there is a head of security who can get hold of backstage passes and tickets for shows that are sold out. Personalised guitar picks were also in great demand and often changed hands for bedroom favours. It may be that not all security men were taking advantage of their position but certainly some of them were not short of female company.

A combination of cocaine and alcohol was always readily available and seemed a necessary element of rock 'n' roll life. In most cases the excesses of yesterday have given way to moderation in middle age. For some such as Eric Clapton, total abstinence has been the key to survival. The iron man of rock, Keith Richards, may still enjoy a bottle of red wine for breakfast but few could have imagined years ago that one day he would be seen in advertisements for Louis Vuitton luggage, the ultimate luxury brand, following in the footsteps of Gorbachev and André Agassi. There were those like Elvis, Hendrix and Cobain, for whom the excesses were too much. But of those who survived many are still going strong.

Back in the '60s, for any rebellious young man from a poor

and underprivileged background, rock opened up the road to fame, easy girls and mind-bending substances. The greatest nightmare for any parent was the thought that their daughter might form an attachment to one of the Rolling Stones – or any number of other rockers. They were loud-mouthed, ill-mannered and dangerous, and they lived only for sex and drugs. Such was the public perception of what was then the new music.

The world is now much changed. The establishment, which once despised rock stars, has embraced them to the extent that they constitute a new nobility. Today it would be considered more than acceptable to marry into a rock star dynasty. The survivors have grown old and with age has come acceptability. We have several knights – Sir Mick Jagger, Sir Paul McCartney, Sir Elton John – and if Bob Geldof, KBE, was a British citizen, in all probability we would have Lord Geldof of Faversham. Along with Sir Bob, as he is loosely known (though incorrectly), Sting, Dave Stewart and Bono have embraced worthy causes to save the planet. They travel the world like missionaries of old, meeting presidents and business leaders to spread their message and raise funds for good causes. Eric Clapton, once addicted to heroin and alcohol, now crusades for Alcoholics Anonymous.

Rock stars are now involved in activities that were once the exclusive domain of the upper classes. Kenny Jones, one time drummer with The Faces and The Who, maintains a polo team at Cowdray Park; Roger Waters, the mastermind behind Pink Floyd, breeds and races thoroughbred horses, as does Ronnie Wood in Ireland; Bill Wyman, ex-Rolling Stone, is an amateur archaeologist and has published a number of books including one on the life of the artist Marc Chagall; Rod Stewart collects pre-Raphaelite art. The list could go on and on. Most of these stars are in their 60s and still rocking. The

Stones are not the only ones to have passed a 40th anniversary. Rod Stewart, the Moody Blues, Eric Clapton, Bob Dylan and Status Quo, to name just a few, are still performing. Neil Diamond is headlining at Glastonbury in his 66th year. In a few years 70th birthdays will be celebrated by many of the current performers. When they hang up their guitars it will not be the end of rock. To paraphrase Winston Churchill, it will not even be the beginning of the end. But it will, perhaps, be the end of the beginning.